PUBLISHING
victorpublishing.co.uk

Get Those Sheep Off The Pitch!

A Life in Non-League football

By Phil Staley

Get Those Sheep Off The Pitch!

A Life in Non-League football

By Phil Staley

Acknowledgements

My thanks to my good friend and ghostwriter of this book, Jon Keighren, for his patience with all my spelling mistakes and misuse of the Queen's English.

Thanks to Rick Heath for having the faith to publish this book and risk his entire professional reputation.

Thanks and much love to my two sons Nicholas and Steven for still speaking to me, despite not seeing me whilst they were young.

A big thankyou to all the non-league clubs for their help and consideration and best wishes to all their personnel who I have turned into overnight celebrities by naming them in this masterpiece.

Thanks to my brother in law Trevor Wood for his help with the pictures. And last, but not least, hugs and kisses to my wife Andrea, daughter Lauren Kate and to our pet whippet Soda for keeping his nose out of the way while I was putting pen to paper.

Contents

Introduction

My non-league management career has had many highs and plenty of lows, lots of laughs and bucket loads of tears, so I thought - why not write it all down on paper? I never set out to take charge of so many clubs during my career - it just happened that way! I hope that all of you who read this book get as much enjoyment out of reading it as I did writing it and remembering some of the great days of the past.

It saddens me to see this great game of football being dictated by a handful of clubs lucky enough to have big financial backers in a game now almost entirely devoid of humour (except for Robbie Savage's hair). So whilst I have tried to describe how some non-league clubs operate, I have attempted to inject a few laughs, to remind people at all levels that football is there to be enjoyed. This is not my life story, but a collection of true stories, which will hit a nerve with anybody who has ever played the Beautiful Game, at any level.

I hope I raise a few smiles and I wish everyone involved in non-league football all the very best for the future, whatever it may bring.

Phil Staley.

Where it all started: Secretary Gareth Jones welcomes me to north Wales

Get Those Sheep Off The Pitch! - Phil Staley

1

Where the hell is Bethesda?

AFTER receiving three injuries in one year, I decided that my playing days would soon be over. Any footballer will tell you that it takes a lot longer for the body to heal as the years catch up with you. But I knew there was no way I could leave the game for good.

Within a few weeks of making my mind up, I noticed an advertisement in the Daily Express, which would change my life forever: "Manager or Player/Manager required for part-time Welsh League side Bethesda Athletic." The first question was obvious. Where the hell is Bethesda?

I got the road atlas out - little did I know how useful that publication would prove over the next few years. After scouring the Welsh pages I found Bethesda, not far from Bangor, so I applied. My reasoning went like this: if I failed as a manager, it was far enough from home that it would not prevent me getting another job in England.

So, I put my CV together for the first time - it took one whole minute. I informed Bethesda's Club Secretary that I was applying for the Player-Manager post and, if they wanted to check on my playing abilities, I was turning out for New Mills at Rhyl the following Tuesday night.

I was a goalkeeper, and on a wet and windy night in Rhyl I conceded three goals in a three-all draw. After the game I showered and changed and headed for the clubhouse when I found my route blocked by four mean looking Welshmen. I feared the worst and started to check on my best possible escape route. I had a tendency during games to talk myself into trouble - I wondered if maybe I had done it again.

I need not have worried as the first one introduced himself as Gareth Jones, Secretary of Bethesda. Alongside him was then-Chairman Tommy Jones, who I later christened Tommy the Wallet. They were accompanied by two more directors, believe it or not, also both called Jones: Gwyn and David. It was still blowing a gale so we disappeared under a section of the tin stand that looked in danger of toppling over at a minute's notice. Gareth did most of the talking, thankfully, because he was the only one I could actually understand with their broad accents.

He said he had been impressed with my performance on the pitch, despite conceding three goals, and the way that I spoke out during the game and he offered me the chance to attend an interview the following Sunday, to be held at their club in Bethesda. All four shook hands with me and said some more things which I didn't understand and I left Rhyl that night wondering what I had let myself in for, but still feeling pleased that I had been offered the interview.

On the Sunday morning, my first wife Sylvia, a true football widow, said it would be a good idea if she accompanied me to the interview, so we could make a day of it. The pair of us quickly sorted out a picnic together and left the house, not sure how long it would take. The interview was booked for three o'clock - we left my hometown of Stockport at ten-thirty.

Four hours later we arrived in Bethesda after a tortuous route along steep country roads, which would put Blackpool's Big Dipper to shame. Sylvia said: "Are you sure you fancy making this journey twice a week?" The omens were not good.

Waiting at the clubhouse entrance was little David Jones who took us into a large, freezing cold snooker room where ten people were seated around a couple of smoke-filled tables. They looked like a bunch of extras from the Godfather.

But I needn't have worried, as the Secretary thanked me for coming and introduced me to the rest of the committee who would eventually decide my immediate managerial destiny. They asked a string of questions during an interview that took an age to complete - their accents were so thick that I could not understand a single word and had to ask them over and over again to repeat themselves. By the end, I managed to work out that the wage bill was £60 per week, plus £12 for me. Now, bear in mind, I had never applied for a managerial post in my life and wage bills were a totally new concept to me: I thanked them enthusiastically and said £60 was fine.

I then sat for ten minutes twiddling my thumbs while they debated the situation in front of me - in Welsh! They finally came to a decision and the Club Secretary announced that they were offering me the job as the new manager of Bethesda Athletic Football Club. If there were any other candidates then I never saw them - the job was offered to me there and then. We all shook hands as I accepted the offer and the Secretary then took me to one side to tell me about all the players registered with Bethesda.

I was handed a list of phone numbers and a piece of paper showing the amount of money paid to each player. Some of them were on £2 per week; others earned £5. I doubt they ever needed the services of Roy Keane's accountant. It turned out that ten of the squad were based in Liverpool. Only three actually came from Bethesda, the other two lived in Colwyn Bay. And then he presented me with another problem - the ex-manager came from Liverpool and the Secretary was concerned that several of the Liverpool-based players might not turn up for the next game, which happened to be against the side at the top of the league. Apparently several players were unhappy about the change of manager.

Two hours later I left Bethesda more confused than when I had arrived! It didn't help when Sylvia started berating me for making the "worst decision of my life" because it would mean I would see even less of her and our sons. At that point I knew I had to make a success of it.

The following night I started to ring round the players on the lengthy list to see what response I could get - let's just say it was mixed. Some said they would definitely NOT be there, one said he'd think about it and five said they would turn up for a couple of pounds more. I told them they could have the money, because I was now getting worried about getting a full side together for my first game in charge.

The most positive reaction came from a player called Geoff Fennar who offered to help me if I needed any assistance with the players, so I asked him to be my assistant - it was the best decision I could have made. Geoff took care of the Liverpool-based players so that I could start gathering up a few useful players in Manchester.

I spent the rest of that week wondering how many players would actually turn up on Saturday for my first ever game as a non-league manager. Over the next couple of days I signed two players from the Manchester area, a lad called Alan Blackhurst and a goalkeeper called Dave Bennett. The only other pre-match preparation I could think of was to calm my nerves with a few pints at my local with some friends.

The big day dawned. I had arranged to meet my cousin Mike Boylin who comes along as a spectator to every game I play. Dave and Alan also arrived at 9am and we set off from Stockport. We arrived at the ground at 1.30pm, just ninety minutes before kick-off, and it was all locked up. The only visible signs of life came from a collection of travellers' caravans right outside the ground. The wind was howling against the metal fence, which shook and rattled with every gust. We parked as far away from the caravans as we could manage and sat and waited. At 2pm I spotted little David Jones - the man with the keys. He unlocked the gates and we followed him into the ground, my new stadium, to be greeted by the sight of a superb playing surface - covered in sheep. David assured me they would be cleared by kick-off.

All of the local players arrived so we made our introductions and then I heard Geoff's car screech to a halt at 2.30pm. The opposition players were already out on the pitch, dodging the sheep and warming up. But Geoff had bad news: four of the Liverpool lads had refused to make the trip, so he had collected a friend called Ian Liversedge who had offered to play. Ian later went on to become physio at Oldham Athletic.

But the horrible truth was starting to dawn - I didn't need Carol Vorderman to do the maths for me - we only had nine players. To make matters worse, one of the lads then told me he was carrying a knock and couldn't play: we were down to eight. The committee had gathered on the touchline, muttering to one another in Welsh, of course, but I could guess what they were saying. I quickly registered me and my cousin as players to get us up to ten. Then the Secretary, Gareth, told me he was also registered: we had a team, of sorts.

There was no time for a team talk so we just got ourselves stripped and out we went to face the league leaders, and as we stepped onto the turf my head was down - my first day in charge had so far been a shambles. We lost 4-1 and it would have been even worse but for some brilliant goalkeeping by Dave Bennett.

Back in the changing room I thanked the players for their hard work and commitment against a good side and told them I would be in touch before the following weekend. My cousin missed this pep talk, as he was lying on a bench in the physio's room with an ice pack round his knee. I walked outside to be confronted immediately by the committee...I feared the worst. Gareth said: "The Chairman would like a word with you." I thought to myself, surely they can't sack me after just one game in charge? Can they?

I went into the office and there was Tommy the Wallet. He stood up and offered me a drink and to my amazement told me he felt my game plan for the day had worked well! He put a £5 note in my hand and said: "Buy yourself a drink on the way home." But there was a sting in the tail. As I left his office he added: "I expect us to be top of the league soon - you've got eight games to turn it around."

The following week I had the phone permanently glued to my ear as I trawled the north west for players who might be available for a game in the Welsh League in exchange for a fiver. It wasn't easy, but I came up with a handful of names. I knew if I could offer £7 to just two players we might have the makings of a decent side. But most players I asked gave me a two-word answer and the second word was always "off."

But eventually I did land a couple of decent lads in Malcolm Torkington and David Royle. But my best signing of all was a minibus from Reddish Car Hire, which would allow me to collect the Manchester players and the Liverpool players in one journey, so we could all travel together.

Our next fixture was away to Bangor University who played within the grounds of the university itself. I collected the minibus at 8.30am then carried on to pick up the Manchester-based players, before heading down to a pub called the Cheshire Yeoman near Queensferry. Not knowing exactly who would be there, Geoff told me he had engaged the services of another player so I was hoping to see five in the car park - to my amazement there were six!

One of them was Dick Morris, who had the unfortunate nickname 'Bacon Face', the result of a nasty car crash - football is a cruel world! But Dick had good contacts on the Wirral, was willing to work for nothing and reckoned he could source some decent players. Dick was well off and didn't need the money so he was hired immediately. He also spoke Welsh, which proved to be a major benefit.

On arrival at the ground I introduced our new players to the Chairman and Secretary and at 2.30pm in my second game in charge I gave my first ever team talk. The game started with a flourish, Alan Blackhurst scoring with his first touch. This was followed up with a real beauty from Geoff Fennar to put us 2-0 up at halftime. Into the second half and with an hour on the clock we were awarded a penalty, which Paul Roberts slotted home to give us a 3-0 victory.

I was on cloud nine until Tommy the Wallet informed me Bangor were bottom of the table and we were expected to beat them anyway. He said: "Next week, it's Porthmadog and they are second in the league.

That'll be a proper test for you."

Despite Tommy's pessimism, I felt a warm glow as I travelled home (although it might only have been the heater in the Transit van) and we talked about the victory and about the future. I had my first win under my belt.

The following week, Dick Morris rang and arranged for us to go and visit a player in Liverpool who Dick rated very highly. He had been on Wrexham's books but had been released in February and was looking for a club. His name was Joey Duncan and it would prove to be a name I never forgot.

Joey signed for us on the Tuesday night for the princely sum of £5 per week and we arranged to pick him up from the Cheshire Yeoman the following Saturday morning. One of the Colwyn Bay players rang me that night to say he was injured, so Joey would have to go straight into the starting line-up on Saturday.

As we set off from the Cheshire Yeoman that Saturday morning, Joey asked if I would take a slight detour via Mold so he could get a message to his brother who worked on the market there. This was well before the days of mobile phones. When we arrived Joey leapt from the minibus and disappeared into the busy stalls for a good twenty minutes. When he finally reappeared he was carrying a huge box full of fresh fruit which his brother had given to him. It was overflowing with apples, oranges, pears, bananas and even halves of melon.

We set off again and almost immediately came to a very steep hill, which needed several gear changes before I could conquer it. The minibus chugged and whined and complained as it started to crawl slowly up this sharp incline. Halfway up I overtook a poor cyclist who was sweating and huffing and puffing as he struggled gamely to pedal up this wicked slope. Suddenly there was pandemonium in the back of the bus. I swung round and saw that Joey had reached out of the window as we went past this poor cyclist and shoved half a melon right into his face.

This unfortunate victim didn't know what had hit him as the Gala Melon landed square in his kisser, he wobbled to the right, then the left, before finally pitching into the hedge at the side of the road. Thankfully the only thing that was hurt was his pride. I drove on, attempting to bollock Joey at the same time, but unfortunately I couldn't stop laughing - it was one of the funniest things I had ever seen - and by this time we were all in hysterics.

We carried on towards Bethesda, but an hour later as we entered Betws y Coed we were stopped by a burly policeman who told me the fruit (which we had already eaten) had been stolen. I told him there was no fruit on the bus, while Joey insisted his brother had given him six oranges and no more. After a few more minutes we were allowed to continue our journey. For the rest of the trip I had one thought in my mind: "This Joey had better be a good player!"

Pre-match I gave my team talk - at this level of football you can never be sure exactly what the players are thinking, so I settled for the usual clichés: "Roll your sleeves up, come on lads, get some fire in your bellies!" It seemed to do the trick as we beat Porthmadog 3-1 and guess who was man-of-the-match? Who else: Joey Duncan. Everyone at the ground was ecstatic - even the committee started speaking in English! I was beginning to think that non-league management was a doddle. Just make sure you have eleven players who will compete in every way possible and you have a good chance of success.

On the way home we stopped at a pub called the Gardeners Arms in Ruthin and spent about an hour there having a few drinks and talking about our second successive victory. On leaving the pub we all piled into the minibus and I had only driven about fifty yards when I spotted the landlord chasing us out of the car park. I couldn't tell exactly what he was saying but it sounded a bit like: "Stop, you thieving bastards!"

The lads yelled at me to drive away - quickly - so I pretended I hadn't seen him, still oblivious to what was happening. A few miles further down the road, I pulled into a garage to get the full story. It transpired that Joey had pinched two brass kettles from the pub fireplace that he intended to flog in Liverpool that night. The next day I rang Dick and told him to go to Joey's house and sack him. Joey's gran had the kettles so he collected them from her and they were returned to the landlord. Just two weeks into my new job and I had to get rid of my first quality player for disciplinary reasons. I wonder if Bill Shankly ever had these kinds of problems?

Despite this hitch, I continued to notch up some good results during the remaining six weeks of the season, losing only one match before the end of the campaign. We finished a creditable fifth in the league, which pleased everyone at the club, but would leave us with a hard act to follow in the forthcoming season.

During the summer, a non-league manager spends most of his time trying to sign new players that he feels are better than the ones he already has. I found myself with nine new faces, but with 22 registered players it would be very difficult to keep everyone happy. In fact, there would be no room in the minibus!

To help me decide, I arranged a couple of pre-season friendlies closer to home so we could have a look at everybody and then pick the twelve that would travel. The club would only pay twelve and Tommy the Wallet could not be persuaded to part with any more cash. I arranged a friendly on the Wirral and then one at Warrington, using all the players over the two games, before selecting the side for our opening fixture at home to Llandudno Swifts. I had signed a local striker called Tony McNelly who was renowned for being late, but even he managed to meet us on time. We were off to a flying start!

And the day just got better and better - by half time we were 8-0 up and we eventually ran out 14-0 winners. Believe it or not, their young goalkeeper had an excellent game - you may have heard of him: Neville Southall. I was so impressed with him, despite the scoreline, that I tapped him up after the game, but he said he had no intention of leaving Llandudno. But he did leave soon after to turn pro with Bury before playing 578 league games for Everton.

We won the next three games in a row to storm to the top of the table, but while the football was going incredibly well, my marriage was starting to show signs of strain. However, I turned a blind eye, buoyed by my own ego, and carried on regardless. After one midweek game at Pwhelli I arrived home at 3.45am before getting up a few hours later to return the minibus before 9am to avoid incurring extra charges.

At the time, I was working full time for British Airways ground staff. It was shift work, which helped a lot because I could swap shifts to accommodate my football. But I found I was rarely at home and my two young sons never saw me. Success was my goal and nothing, not even my family, would get in my way. As a team we were doing very well and winning was becoming second nature for us. By Christmas we were still top of the league and still in three cup competitions.

But the start of the New Year brought my first big disappointment as we crashed out of the Welsh Cup at the hands of a team we had beaten only two weeks earlier. This day sticks in my mind because on the way to the game we were involved in a minor road accident, which held us up for half an hour, but thankfully no-one was seriously injured. At the final whistle you could sense the disappointment around the ground and for the first time in months I saw the committee go into their huddle and start speaking Welsh again. But my biggest worry was losing my deposit for the damage to the minibus.

But we still had a lot to play for and our next game was away to the great Freddie Pye's side Nantile Vale. We kept faith with the same eleven, but on arrival at the ground found ourselves in the world's smallest changing room. It would have been impossible to house two Dwarf Netherland rabbits, let alone a football team. Two coat pegs on one side, three on the other and a bench down the middle. But we didn't let it affect our performance - by half-time we were 3-0 up and at the final whistle were celebrating a 5-1 victory. To make things even better we heard that second-placed Porthmadog had lost to Rhyl giving us a four-point lead at the top of the table.

Arriving home at 11.30 that evening, my wife had taken the boys round to her parents' house for the night so I had plenty of time to ponder our famous victory. It never occurred to me that my family would not be coming home tomorrow.

I was hooked on winning and carried on regardless of the impact on my home life. The side went from strength to strength taking maximum points from the next five games leaving us seven points clear with Easter on the horizon. We had a blank weekend so I decided to arrange a friendly to keep the lads on their toes. I hired a ground in Birkenhead and we invited Nantwich Town to take us on, managed by the late Alan Ball. At every game that Nantwich played, Alan would be accompanied by his son Alan Ball Junior. Alan Senior said we should go for a pint after the game in the great City of Liverpool so, soon after the final whistle, we piled back onto the minibus and made our way to the entrance of the Mersey Tunnel. We paid our toll and entered the tunnel followed by Alan Ball, his son and two of his players.

Halfway through, the bus conked out and, after several attempts to restart it, we gave up. Alan pulled round to the front of the minibus, found a thick rope in the boot of his car and towed us to the Liverpool end of the Mersey Tunnel where we finally managed to call the AA. To our amazement, the following weekend when we arrived in Bethesda we read the following story in the local paper: "After last weekend's friendly fixture in Birkenhead, the whole of the Bethesda team had to be towed out of the Mersey Tunnel by the Balls!"

Easter weekend came and we were facing Pwhelli away: second versus first. Victory would put us ten points clear at the top. There was a good-sized but hostile crowd for this one and we were subjected to several obscenities as we arrived at the ground. We had been warned that Welsh Nationalists might try to infiltrate the crowd and use the occasion to have a go at our English players.

The warm welcome continued inside the ground where we entered the changing room to be greeted with the strong stench of urine - to make it worse several people had crapped on the floor and left the evidence behind. The light was minimal and there was a sign warning us not to leave any valuables in the changing room. On the wall, written in chalk, were the words: "Welcome to Hell." It made Galatasaray look like Butlins.

We got ourselves organised as best we could in the tiny changing room, dodging the turds on the floor. There was a constant banging on the walls from the supporters outside. I took the decision that we would dispense with our usual warm-up on the pitch and we opted to stay inside until taking to the field just in time for the kick-off.

It felt as if we were playing in a bear pit, but we reached the break all square at nil-nil. The referee asked if we wanted to go inside at half time but I decided it would be safer to stay on the field rather than run the gauntlet of the Welsh Nationalists hanging over the wall near the tunnel entrance. I gathered the lads in the centre circle because this was as far away from the crowd as we could possibly get! No tea, no oranges, but we were receiving plenty of abuse from the sidelines.

Into the second half and the game remained goalless until the 87th minute when the home side won a corner. Keeper Dave Bennett emerged from a ruck of players with the ball and, to our amazement, the referee awarded a penalty. Despite our protests the decision stood and Pwhelli successfully converted the spot-kick and hung on to claim all three points.

After the final whistle the abuse from the crowd continued but I was deaf to this as I was busy hurling my own volley of abuse at the referee. Two weeks later I regretted it: I was fined £50 by the Welsh FA and warned about my future conduct.

Because we were playing Porthmadog on Easter Monday, Tommy the Wallet agreed to find us suitable accommodation for the team to stay over in Wales throughout the weekend. We were told that three guesthouses had been booked for us for the Saturday and Sunday evenings. The trip back to Bethesda was a bit low key but I did my best to lift the lads' spirits by promising them a good Saturday night out in North Wales. I hoped this was not a contradiction in terms.

Arriving back in Bethesda we were shocked to discover the state of our lodgings for the next two nights. Tommy the Wallet had certainly not stretched his budget and I could not help laughing when I saw the expressions on the lads' faces. I was lucky: I was staying with Secretary Gareth Jones, which turned out to be a smart move as our rooms were not too bad. For the players, it was a different story.

The landlady of one house decided to give a couple of the lads a guided tour of her shanty-style 'B & B' so I felt duty-bound to join them. I had tears in my eyes as she proudly showed us a series of filthy, poky rooms which she seemed to think deserved five stars. All you could hear as you walked around the property was a "squelch, squelch" as your feet stuck to some unidentifiable stains on the lino. I told the lads to stop complaining - after all, this was their first trip into Europe!

On Monday, we left the town and headed for Porthmadog's picturesque ground nestling under the Snowdonia Mountains. This was a far better atmosphere than we had experienced on Saturday and I decided it would be a lot easier for me to keep my cool this tim2111111e. The players must have slept well at their "luxury" accommodation in Bethesda because their workrate was excellent and we ran out worthy 2-0 winners. More good news followed as we heard that Pwhelli had been held to a draw by Nantile Vale, leaving us six points clear at the top.

The travelling was becoming very arduous but the thought of winning the league and cup double kept me going. There was also an added bonus of being manager of Bethesda - groundsman Wyn Jones. Wyn was a chubby red-faced character who not only kept the playing surface in excellent condition, but after every home game presented me with a bin liner full of fresh salmon, which he caught himself on the River Ogwen that ran alongside the ground. Tragically Wyn died in a car crash right outside the ground just days before we completed the double, winning five in a row at the end of the season before beating Porthmadog 3-0 in the North Wales cup final.

It was tinged in sadness, but my first season as a non-league manager had ended in triumph and the feeling was unbelievable. My thoughts were that some club nearer to home might take notice and offer me a job as a result of my achievements in North Wales. Clubs around Manchester seem to change their managers with alarming regularity so I felt that during the close season I might get an offer I could not refuse.

Despite our success at Bethesda, the travelling had

started to take its toll and I also felt I could find a better standard of player in my own neck of the woods, rather than have to persuade them to make an eight-hour round trip for a game of football. It would also allow me to spend more time with my family who had reluctantly returned home still bemoaning my frequent absences.

In the end, I did move on, but I never forgot my first club who gave me a chance to prove my capabilities as a non-league manager.

The sheep keep the grass short in Bethesda!

Caravans in the car park at Bethesda.

Bethesda's championship side. I'm the windswept one on the right!

Get Those Sheep Off The Pitch! - Phil Staley

The luxury changing rooms at Bethesda!

Get Those Sheep Off The Pitch! - Phil Staley

2

The day I signed Manchester United's Boy Wonder

It had been a long, hard season and it was time for a break so I decided to take the family to Sitges for a fortnight on the Spanish mainland. I felt on top of the world after winning the league and cup double in Wales and I felt that we all deserved a break after twelve months of ups and downs.

But we'd only got as far as the departure lounge at Manchester Airport when football came back to the fore. An old friend Jimmy Golder was there, a man with an encyclopaedic knowledge of the non-league scene. He told me there were several jobs likely to come up during the summer months that would suit me and promised to keep his ear to the ground.

I had to break off the discussion as I could see the steam start to emerge from Sylvia's ears. As I rejoined the family, she said: "Bloody football - you just can't get away from it, can you? Even when we are going on holiday!"

But things were about to get even worse. As we boarded the plane I spotted a guy called Vinnie Townley, a midfield player who I was hoping to sign for the new season. I didn't let my wife know, but I made sure I sat on the aisle so I could get up easily and move around the cabin.

45 minutes into the flight, Vinnie's wife got up to go to the loo - I spotted my chance to move in. I shot up and moved down the cabin like a gazelle before planting myself next to the man I wanted to sign for the forthcoming campaign, whether I was managing Bethesda or not.

I spent a long time outlining my plans - Vinnie's wife came back and had to sit across the aisle while we continued our transfer talks. We even ordered a round of drinks as I set out my own agenda for the coming season. Three drinks later, I returned to my seat after securing a verbal commitment from this very useful midfielder. Sylvia just glared at me. There really was no escape from football. The remainder of the flight to Alicante passed in silence.

Things picked up when we arrived at the resort as I managed to organise a game of football between the guests and the hotel staff. We got a great response from the guests and thirteen of them signed up for the match. The staff team had an old playing strip that had been handed down over the years, but the guests had nothing to wear for the big match.

The Friday morning before the game I headed off to the local market with a lad called Graham to see if we could get a few shirts for our side. The lads all chipped in a few pesetas each to buy the most hideous, flimsy green T-shirts available. But even whilst preparing for this fun game my mind was already thinking about the chance of spotting a player or two that might be available for next season! I just couldn't switch off.

We agreed a kick-off time of 9.30am because of the searing Spanish heat and to fit in with the staff rosters. We commandeered the hotel transfer bus, which would ferry us to the chosen venue, which no one had yet clapped eyes on.

The early start put paid to the chances of everyone turning up - two were missing but at least we could still field a full side. The courtesy bus left the hotel and we arrived at the ground: we immediately dubbed it "The Stadium of Shite". To call it ramshackle would be a massive understatement.

The pitch itself looked like one of those old tennis courts made out of red shale, there were no markings and the goal posts were a couple of drain pipes stuck in the ground. The only boundary markings of any description were four buckets - we eventually realised that they were the corner flags.

There we were, kitted out in our snot green T-shirts, the temperature already nudging 90 degrees, but we were there and ready to play. Within ten minutes we were two goals down with three players already limping from the unforgiving surface. Dehydration started to set in and by halftime we were on the wrong end of a 6-0 scoreline. 45 minutes later we were down to eight men and the scoreline read 13-1; we were lucky to get the one. My first game in Europe had been a disaster!

The rest of the holiday passed off peacefully as I tried to ease my aching bones. We returned home after a fortnight to find that things at home were moving on at a rapid pace. There was a message on the answer machine from Roy Donnelly, the Chairman of Ashton United, asking me to get in touch as soon as possible. As Sylvia dragged the suitcases out of the car, I was already on the phone making a call that would change my life.

Roy Donnelly was big in seafood - he and his wife Stella had built up a thriving business after deciding to abandon their careers as teachers.

During the call, we agreed to meet up two days later at Hurst Cross, the home of Ashton United. I did not sleep for the next two nights until the appointed time for my interview to become the next manager of this famous Cheshire League side.

Ken Murrie, the Club Secretary, introduced me to Mr Donnelly, who turned out to be a tiny figure of a man - after speaking on the phone I had expected to be confronted by a strapping six-foot frame but he was quite the opposite. But what he lacked in height, he made up for in ambition. He had major plans for the football club and it became clear during the interview he had already done his homework on me.

Within the hour he was offering me the post of manager at Ashton United. It took me a lot less than an hour to accept. We agreed a wage bill, which was considerably higher than my previous one at Bethesda, and he doubled my salary. It was evident he wanted success - and quickly.

The Chairman went on to tell me that only six players had been retained for the forthcoming season, so I would have to get my little black book out and get to work that night. My first job, though, was to try and appoint Geoff Fennar as my assistant after his loyalty at Bethesda. Thankfully he agreed to join me at Ashton, which would mean we had a good chance of attracting the top players from Merseyside once again.

My second task would be to make the hardest phone call of my life: ringing Tommy the Wallet to tell him I would not be returning to Bethesda for the new season. To my surprise, he was very calm and wished me all the best in my new capacity and thanked me for what we had achieved at Bethesda.

For the next few hours I was on Cloud Nine. No more travelling to the back of beyond in North Wales - and a chance to prove myself in the north west of

England. One other person I needed to appoint was Dick Morris, my chief scout and top poacher of players from other non-league clubs. He agreed to join me, so the management team was complete.

The next fortnight was a frenzy of activity as we signed 16 players in just 14 days. Barry Fry would have been proud of me! Pre-season training began in earnest with a collection of talented young players. We had signed a terrific goalkeeper straight from Stockport County called Ian Holbrook, there was a centre half from St Helens called Barrie Lowe and a tall gangly centre forward from Liverpool called Terry O'Connor, who was built in the mould of Ian Rush. These three would prove to be the backbone of the side.

We also brought in a sweeper from Warrington called Colin Hope, although everyone knew him by the name of Whopper - I'll leave you to guess why. A lad called Tony Keyes held the midfield together. We called him Desert Orchid because of his wispy white and grey hair.

We then made a big signing by non-league standards by picking up the former Stockport County and Manchester City striker Barney Daniels. It made headline news in the local newspaper at the time with Barney still a big name in the north-west. We felt that his experience, plus his goalscoring record, would give the side a massive lift.

Ten games into the season, things were going well: seven wins, two draws and just one defeat. But the Chairman, in typical fashion, was not happy with the one defeat. He felt we needed to strengthen the side even more. Mr Donnelly had read in the paper that the former England schoolboy international Peter Coyne was unhappy at Manchester United and wanted to leave Old Trafford. Mr Donnelly said he knew Peter well from his schoolboy days and reckoned he could persuade him to come to Ashton. You can imagine my reaction - the equivalent today would be Altrincham attempting to sign Jesper Blomqvist!

But Mr Donnelly was adamant. He had taught Peter Coyne at school and he knew Peter enjoyed the odd flutter now and again. The Chairman suggested he could attract Peter by offering him a full-time job selling seafood: cockles, mussels, kippers and prawns - I cannot imagine Jesper Blomqvist taking on this kind of job. But Mr Donnelly was prepared to offer Peter Coyne the job, a van and £200 per week - as long as he played for Ashton United.

Peter had appeared to have a bright future ahead of him in the game. As a schoolboy he had scored a hat trick for England against Germany at Wembley, a performance that earned him a four-year contract at Old Trafford. Our Mr Donnelly was trying to pull off the biggest transfer deal in the history of non-league football, while the boy still had two years of this contract remaining. To make matters worse, Bolton Wanderers had already offered Coyne a new three-year deal to move to Burnden Park.

But the Chairman was persistent and to my astonishment he rang me to say he had arranged a private meeting with Peter Coyne for the following Tuesday night at a pub in Gorton on the outskirts of Manchester. I could not believe my ears - why would a full-time professional at Manchester United want to leave Old Trafford and move to tiny Ashton United? I assumed the Chairman had lost his marbles and moved to Fantasy Island.

But 6.30pm the following Tuesday on a wet and windy night I arrived at the pub for this incredible rendezvous with the United starlet. It became clear that Peter's love for football was eclipsed by the only other love in his life: gambling. Peter would have had a bet on two flies crawling up a wall. Donnelly knew that the lure of a van, cash in his hand and a golden handshake might just be enough to tempt Peter Coyne away from the Theatre of Dreams.

We spent just 45 minutes discussing the boy's future - Peter terminated the discussion by saying he wanted 48 hours to think it over. He had to dash off because he wanted to catch the 7.53pm race up the road at Belle Vue dog track.

As I drove home that night there was just one word I could think of to describe this youngster who seemingly had the world at his feet: stupid. But from a purely selfish point of view I knew it could catapult Ashton United into the big time. The publicity would be unprecedented and the results on the pitch could be phenomenal with someone this talented in our line-up.

The next afternoon I got the call: Peter Coyne had gone in to see Tommy Docherty, the manager of Manchester United, and told him he wanted to leave Old Trafford and cancel his contract with the Reds. He told Docherty he wanted to give up full-time football for a more stable career - selling seafood.

The following night the Chairman rang to say that ITV's Friday night football show wanted me, Peter Coyne and Mr Donnelly to appear live on the programme to talk about this ridiculous move from Manchester United to Ashton United. I was instructed to wear my best suit, shirt and tie for the show. It was by far the biggest story to come out of Old Trafford at that time.

We had already been tipped off by Peter Coyne's brother Ged that their father was very unhappy about our approach for his son and he had gone on to make it quite clear via the Manchester Evening News that he would do everything in his power to stop the move going through.

Undeterred, Roy Donnelly decided it would be a great idea if we got Peter to sign his Ashton United forms live on television, as this would help to give the club even greater exposure. The Chairman picked me up at 5.30pm on the night of the show - Peter Coyne was already with him and he seemed quite happy about the whole affair.

But we were in for a shock on our arrival at Granada Television. Up on the third floor just minutes before we were due to go on air we were confronted by Peter's father who was waiting for us to arrive. Not surprisingly, he homed in on me: "You bastard," he yelled, "You are going to ruin my son's career."

I paused, unsure of what to do, but decided I would try to discuss the matter in a calm and adult fashion. Then he lunged at me and swung a punch that struck a glancing blow across the side of my head. At this stage two security guards moved in, split us up and sent us off to separate rooms.

There was another shock to come - the producers told me they would not need me on camera after all - they had decided to use Peter's father instead. This was the guy who was totally opposed to the transfer and had just tried to knock seven bells out of me. Granada were hoping to have an explosive live event on TV with Peter trying to sign the forms, while his father tried to prevent him. This whole fiasco was threatening to blow up in our faces on live television. I was told it would be a good idea if I went home to avoid any further conflict.

I was gutted: thirty quid for a new shirt, twenty pounds for a new tie and a whole afternoon spent shining my shoes, all for nothing. I was less than half an hour away from my first ever TV appearance and being involved in the biggest non-league transfer coup the football world had ever seen. But I knew I could not go home - after all, the Chairman was giving me a lift back - so I had to head off to the nearest bar to drown my sorrows. Luckily the bar had a TV so I prepared to watch the drama unfold.

It did not take long. Peter's dad was visibly fuming, getting redder and redder by the second. Within seconds of the item starting, he was venting his fury on Roy Donnelly, our Chairman. Roy talked a good fight and stuck up for himself, defending his actions in poaching this young star from Old Trafford. Sadly, it was left to Peter himself to try and explain to his father why he had decided to swap a life at the world's biggest football club for a career selling seafood. He also had to explain why he had rejected the offer of a contract from Bolton Wanderers.

After much argument and heated debate, the forms were signed live on Granada, in a deal that I have to admit I did not like at all. But the following weekend, Peter was introduced to the rest of the squad. The Chairman insisted Peter should go straight into the side, but I decided it would be better for him to take a look at what he was letting himself in for. Half an hour before kick-off I told Peter I wanted him to sit out the first game, taking into consideration we had been on a pretty successful run even before his arrival.

The Chairman was not happy. He called me outside and explained that they were anticipating a bumper four-figure crowd, all turning up to see Coyne in action. He told me: "This is one decision you will not be making. Peter Coyne will make his debut for Ashton United this afternoon." I had no choice and had to drop one of my strikers to make way for the new boy wonder. But the whole incident had affected me badly. Geoff Fennar came over and had a word with me, advising me to forget about it and get on with the game.

Peter had a very quiet debut and, at times, looked like a fish-seller out of water. He just could not cope with being kicked in the air by the opposition centre half, who happened to be the former Liverpool legend big Ron Yeats. Peter left the field looking like a bilberry tart - black and blue all over.

After a couple more games, I decided Peter needed a break and it proved to be a sign of things to come. I used him sparingly throughout the remainder of the season and his form was erratic to say the least. The team continued to pick up points, but it was more often than not when Peter was left out of the starting line-up. But to be fair, on a number of occasions, he did show his true class so I made it my intention to try and get the boy back to where he should be - in League football.

It was a great relief to everyone when Peter was eventually offered a trial at Crewe Alexandra, not only because we got rid of the smell of fish from the changing room, but because Peter was finally getting the chance to shine again in professional football. He scored 47 goals in 153 games for Crewe before ending his career with Swindon and Aldershot.

A check of Manchester United's official website shows Peter's name still up there in lights, but the records show he made just two appearances for the first team, scoring one goal.

As a junior at Old Trafford he had been scoring goals for fun. But betting was a big part of Coyne's life even in his early days at Manchester United. At the start of the 1975-76 campaign, Coyne bet £5 with Tommy Docherty that he would score 40 goals in that season. By February he had Docherty's money: in all teams from the 'B' side through to the League team, Coyne notched up 45 goals. But ManUtd.com reveals: "Sadly, he never realised his full potential and his United contract was cancelled in March 1977."

The Coyne incident proved to be my final clash with Ashton Secretary Ken Murrie. For some reason, Ken and I never saw eye-to-eye during my time at Ashton United. There had been a clash of personalities virtually from Day One. He even seemed happy when

I ran into trouble with the football authorities. I can still remember the great delight on his face one time when he told me that I had been summonsed to appear before the Manchester FA the following Wednesday night after my third sending-off as a manager. Ken gloated and remarked: "They'll throw the key away this time, Staley!" Charming.

But I have to admit I was a bit worried about the whole thing as my disciplinary record was not good, and my intolerance towards officials was renowned. I knew this could potentially have a devastating effect on my career. This latest run-in with officialdom would be costly.

But then a close friend, Len Joyce, offered to provide me with a false alibi. Len said he would go before the Manchester FA and tell them that I wasn't even at the ground on the day of the game when I "allegedly" received my marching orders. In hindsight it was a ludicrous idea, but it worked. I had attended a birthday party at Len's house the night before the game. Len's plan was to produce a photograph of me from the party, which had in fact been taken some FOUR MONTHS EARLIER.

The picture showed me to be clean-shaven - on the Saturday of the sending off I had a full beard. Len said that his evidence would be enough to clear me on the grounds of mistaken identity! The case would hinge on the fact that I could not have grown a full beard overnight. I decided to give it a go.

I shaved well before Len and I attended the FA hearing. We arrived with ten minutes to spare and sat down outside the office, next to the very referee who had sent me off. It was Kevin Lynch, who went on to become one of the nation's top referees and a good friend, as well. We sat outside for several minutes and it became apparent that Mr Lynch did not have a clue who I was without the beard!

We were eventually called inside to face a panel of five FA officials. The Chairman of the Sitting Commission outlined the case against me. My defence was a pack of lies. I told the panel that referee Lynch had been approached at halftime by an individual who hurled a volley of abuse at him. This person then gave him my name instead of their own. I told the Commission that in the referee's report it quite clearly stated that the person he sent off had a full beard and was wearing glasses - of course, I had dispensed with the glasses as well as the beard for the hearing!

Just five minutes into the hearing, referee Lynch interrupted the discussion and told the Commission that I was NOT the person he sent off that Saturday afternoon at Ashton United Football Club. The Commission dismissed the case and I left the hearing shaking the hand of Mr Lynch.

I thought I had got away with it, but my relief was premature. Unfortunately my good friend Len let the story slip to someone at work and word of my indiscretion got back to Ashton Secretary Ken Murrie. He fired off a letter to the County FA explaining the con in detail and I was hauled back in front of them for a second time. However, Len and I stuck to our story and the Commission was unable to prove that I was in fact the guilty party on that day, so with no further evidence they were forced to abandon the case against me.

I explained to them the nature of the relationship between myself and Secretary Murrie, who it seemed had the knife in for me from the day I arrived at Ashton United. In the end, Murrie was warned about his future conduct and the club itself was hit with a fine for £150. Murrie was asked to tender his resignation, but the whole affair had left a nasty taste in the mouth and I decided it was time to move on to pastures new.

In disguise! My beard fools the County FA.

Get Those Sheep Off The Pitch! - Phil Staley

3

Joining the Macc Lads

It was a fairly grim end to the season as I parted company not only with Ashton United, but also my right-hand man Geoff Fennar. Geoff had decided to take a fulltime position with his company, which necessitated a move overseas to Boston in the United States of America. It turned out to be a major blow to my own football ambitions.

After my departure from Ashton I was out of work for literally a few hours. The non-league grapevine must have been working overtime because I was swiftly offered a job at Chorley FC as first team coach, working alongside their highly regarded manager Alan Spence.

Alan and I had known each other for a long time and I felt this post would give me the chance to work more closely with the players, as well as giving me more time to spend with my family. I took on the job and it worked out well for me and it looked as though I would have a settled time ahead of me at Chorley.

Three weeks into my tenure at the club, I was sitting in the big old stone bath at the Victory Ground when the Chorley Secretary shouted through to say there was a telephone call for me. Now, it was a rare event for me to receive a phone call. Since taking a coaching role as opposed to managing, calls at the ground were few and far between.

I grabbed the club's tiniest bath towel and clutched it as best I could, covering anything that moved, as I ran down the freezing cold corridor to the Secretary's office. I answered the phone and heard Macclesfield Town Chairman Alan Brocklehurst at the other end.

Alan told me he was in the middle of a board meeting at their Moss Rose ground having just parted company with their manager. He said: "The directors and I were just wondering if you would be interested in coming for an interview tomorrow evening?"

Macclesfield, of course, were a club on the up, only a few years short of making their debut in the Football League. At that time, the Silkmen were one of the biggest names in non-league football and it took me all of two seconds to agree to Alan's request. We arranged to meet at the ground at 8pm.

I returned to the warmth of the stone bath, literally shaking (mainly because I'd lost my towel on the way back). The thought of becoming manager of Macclesfield in only my fourth season in non-league football made the hairs stand up on the back of my neck. It was like my first day at school, my first kiss, my first job interview and my first wedding day - all rolled into one!

As I finally emerged from the water, like the Man from Atlantis, I felt ten feet tall. I went to get changed. Most of the lads had left by this time so the changing room was empty. Out of courtesy, I decided I should go and speak to the manager as early as possible, to explain what had happened.

Alan Spence was a true gent, and he was genuinely delighted for me and wished me all the best for the following evening's interview. He admitted it was the sort of job that any non-league manager would dream of landing. I intended to give it my best shot.

I had a fulltime job, so I decided to take the afternoon off before the interview, to make sure I was fully prepared and in the right frame of mind. I arrived at the Moss Rose in plenty of time and sat in my car to kill the last ten minutes before I was due in the boardroom. It was the longest ten minutes of my life as I nervously went through all the things I wanted to say.

Inside, I was introduced to the club's six directors who said they had heard of my reputation for spotting good talent and securing that talent on contracts. The interview didn't last too long, thankfully, and a short time later I found myself waiting in another room while they made their deliberations. I only had to wait a few minutes before I was summoned back into the boardroom to be told that the job was mine, if I wanted it.

For some reason, it actually crossed my mind to ask for 24 hours to consider the offer! But I was terrified that any delay would give them time to change their minds, so I accepted the job there and then. The board must have been confident that I would accept because they had already arranged a press conference at the ground. Within minutes, the local press were there and I spent a good hour talking to them about my hopes and ambitions for Macclesfield Town.

On the way home, I stopped to fill up with petrol, before realising I had left my wallet at home amidst all the excitement. I did not have a single penny on me, so went into the shop to explain my predicament to the cashier. She told me I would have to fill in several forms.

I said: "There's no problem, I've just been appointed manager of Macclesfield Town so I will be passing here again tomorrow. Can I just drop the money off then?" She replied: "I don't care if you're the manager of England, you're still filling these forms in."

The following evening I met the players for the first time. They were all good non-league stalwarts such as Dave Mobley, Joe Fletcher, Dave Carrick, Gary Blore and Robin Simpson. Robin was called "lamb chop" because he would never shut up - his chops were never closed.

But I would also need a new backroom staff having lost Geoff Fennar and Dick Morris who had both gone overseas with their jobs. On this first night I asked Joe and Dave to take our debut training session, as they were the two most senior players. That gave me the chance to make a few phone calls in preparation for my opening fixture at the Brendan Foster Stadium up at Gateshead on the following Saturday.

Gateshead has always been a tricky away fixture and it was made even more difficult for Macclesfield because of the managerial change and the side's lack of confidence.

I had been given some useful information, though, about a guy who was running the Cheshire Youth side called Jimmy Williams. One of the players I intended taking with me from Ashton United had recommended Jimmy very highly, so I gave him a call. Jimmy was a broad scouser, but I liked him straight away and offered him the post of Assistant Manager, on a trial basis initially. He said: "F**king great!"

Before Saturday, I intended to sign a couple of new players to strengthen the side, but I still asked everyone in the current squad to turn up for the trip to the north east. I was relieved that Jimmy had agreed to come on board because, for once, I was without a right-hand man. It also meant I could keep up my links with Liverpool where Jimmy was based and still attract some good players from Merseyside.

I made a couple of signings that week and we headed north in good spirits - we returned even happier having won 1-0 to claim maximum points. Rob Wheeler scored the only goal of the game, in Macclesfield's first win of the season.

Over the next few weeks we chopped and changed the starting line-up, it was a well-known fact that I liked to bring in my own players so I made it quite clear that there was not room for everyone and one or two players would have to drop out.

At this time, I had just bought a second-hand van from my fulltime employers, British Airways and because it was red, white and blue we called it Concorde. Like all managers at that level of football, it was my job to make sure all the players got to the games on time, even if it meant picking them up yourself. I have even known some of the game's top managers do it, like Dario Gradi at Crewe, never afraid to get his hands dirty.

On one occasion we were returning home after a game at the Moss Rose and I pulled up in Stockport to drop off a couple of our players, leaving just me and one other player in Concorde. As I pulled away from the kerb, a Ford Capri came across my path and I clipped the side of his door. I have to confess I had had a couple of drinks earlier on, so I suggested we pull round the corner to sort this out.

He turned into the next road, while I put my foot down and tore off towards the town centre, leaving the scene of the crime before he had time to reverse back onto the main road. But I knew the driver would already have taken down my registration number - and the van was hardly the most anonymous vehicle on the highway! I decided there was just one option: paint it white.

A few weeks later, one Sunday morning, there was a knock at the door - there were two police officers standing outside right next to Concorde. One of them asked: "Is this your van?" I told them it was mine, but then he asked: "Has it always been white?" The questions were getting a bit trickier now, so I invited them both inside for a cup of tea. They explained that a van with my numberplate had been involved in an accident and they started to quiz me about how long I had owned the vehicle.

Then all of a sudden, the older officer asked: "Are you Phil Staley, the manager of Macclesfield Town?" Well, my eyes lit up: he was a big non-league fan and knew all about my days at Ashton, including the Peter Coyne story, so I moved the conversation swiftly onto football. After a few more cups of tea and more football chat he said: "OK, Phil, well it was good to meet you. You won't hear any more about this incident." Case closed!

On the field we had a few narrow escapes, as well, with a mixed bag of results as we continued to chop and change the side in a bid to get the right balance. But results were mixed to say the least and I just began to wonder if I may have hit the top in non-league football just a bit too early.

But despite being a big name in non-league football, Macclesfield had its financial difficulties, like any other club at that level. It was very much a hand to mouth existence and we relied greatly on the generosity of many individuals and local companies to keep the thing going. Everyone had to get involved in fund raising, and the manager was no exception. I remember one particular occasion when the club arranged a sponsored walk from Macclesfield to Leek.

Around half a dozen players turned up along with 50 supporters and we set off on this very sunny Sunday lunchtime. I was wlaking with a lad called Jeff Rafferty, a good-looking lad who managed to attract all the women, so he was always a useful guy to know. Jeff and I decided that it would be a good idea to stop for a quick drink at every pub on the route. Eventually, the group became more and more strung out as Jeff and I stuck to our plan to visit every hostelry along the way.

By the time we arrived at Leek it was pitch black. The pub where we were due to finish the walk had long since closed and everyone had left - there wasn't a single car in the car park. Jeff and I were stranded and we had to order a taxi to pick us up and take us home. The taxi fare came to three times the amount we had raised in sponsorship.

Back on the pitch we were due to travel to Stafford Rangers in something of a local derby. The late Roy Chapman, father of Lee Chapman, managed Stafford at the time and it was a daunting task as they were top of the table and playing extremely well. Ahead of this fixture we had just signed one of Stafford's players, a guy called Phil Marsden, for a fee of £400 to be paid up front so he would be eligible for the fixture. Also in the side was Kenny Higham, a big centre-half from Jimmy's neck of the woods. I had also paid Altrincham a nominal fee for Mike Sherlock, a goalkeeper of real quality, who had represented the English Universities side on numerous occasions. This meant that "Lamb Chop" wasn't too happy, so he was allowed to leave the club.

The game was played on a glorious sunny afternoon on a surface more in keeping with crown green bowls than football. After 45 minutes our new look side had competed very well, which made the half-time team talk a lot easier for me with the scoreline still blank.

Into the second half and with just two minutes left the whole complexion of the game was altered. Stafford's right winger floated a deep cross into the six yard box and Sherlock, who had been faultless all afternoon, caught the ball but was barged in the back by the Ranger's centre forward. The ball dropped loose and, with Mike lying injured, their number six Tony Keyes slammed it into the empty net. To our horror, the referee allowed the goal to stand and the crowd of around 900 went wild.

I could not believe it and started remonstrating with the linesman in front of me but all he could say was: "Sit!" I yelled back: "I'm not a flaming dog!" But all he did was laugh and turn away. We had been robbed in the dying seconds, which would have upset even the most placid of managers. Our keeper managed to finish the game but I was livid and had to get it off my chest. I stormed over to the referee on the final whistle to ask why the goal had not been disallowed. He went red and refused to comment, which made me even angrier. I called him a joke and a cheat and accused him of being a "homer". Jimmy alongside me had to be restrained by our trainer Dave Twigg. By now, police and stewards had joined our little cluster in front of the main stand and it was clear we were getting nowhere.

I returned to our silent dressing room where you could have heard a pin drop. I told the lads to forget about it and assured them I hadn't finished with that referee just yet. I gave the officials time to get changed and some twenty minutes later knocked on their door demanding a full explanation about the winning goal, but he still refused to comment. The only thing he said was that he was going to report me to the FA for my comments and bad behaviour. I had to be dragged away before the list of offences grew even longer.

Sure enough, three weeks later I was fined £150 and warned about my future conduct. It was the third time I had been hit with a hefty fine in my short career costing me a total of almost three hundred quid, a lot more than I could afford at a time when I was going out socialising virtually every night. My life consisted of drinking, training and watching games - usually in that order.

Over the next two weeks I made my best ever signing - he didn't do that much on the park but he improved my private life no end! I landed the signature of the former Manchester City player Keith Mason. Now Mase did have some talent on the pitch, but he was an expert at attracting women.

On one particular Saturday night after playing up at Netherfield and collecting three points, as well, Jimmy suggested that Mase, myself and Kenny Higham should all head off to Liverpool's best-known night-spot, the Grafton. It was rough and ready, there was always a fight and never any nice girls in there. In fact, it was the biggest pick-up joint in the north-west of England. So much so, that it was always packed and there was always a queue to get in.

We decided to sleep over at Jimmy's place that night,

so we got changed and set off for the bright lights of Liverpool. We had a couple of pints at Jimmy's local in Kirkby before catching a cab to the Grafton and, sure enough, there was a long line of punters waiting to get in. Jimmy, being a scally, knew someone who was quite near the front and so we all followed him and managed to blag our way into the queue.

Ten minutes later we spotted our first blood donor of the night as two guys started kicking off - within seconds one was still standing, but the other was pole-axed holding his cherry red nose. But this didn't put us off and we paid our money and entered this den of iniquity. It was the sort of place where you would never go for a pee on your own. It was so rough they used to search you on the way in to see if you had any weapons - if you didn't they gave you some!

Mase, who had only made one appearance for Macclesfield so far, was soon making his mark in the night-club and within ten minutes had a group of talent spotters all over him like a rash. They just seemed to creep up on him, like old age! He was grinning from ear to ear, but the biggest laugh of the night was still to come.

Mase had spotted one particularly attractive young lady and was steadily casting the others to one side as he made a beeline for this girl. Kenny, Jimmy and I were left sitting at a table on our own, but we were still within earshot of our newest signing. We heard him offer to walk this girl home and she replied: "But I live in Crosby - that's on the other side of Liverpool!"

Mase had no idea about the geography of Merseyside and replied: "That's no problem. What's a few miles when you're in love?" We were sitting there laughing into our beer at the audacity of the guy, which did not go down well with the new love of Mase's life. Sure enough, he left with this girl on his arm and returned to Jimmy's house in the wee small hours of the morning to tell us he had been forced to beat a hasty retreat when her husband returned unexpectedly from a weekend away with the local pigeon club.

By now my marriage was crumbling around my ears as my long-suffering wife had just about had her fill of my football career and all it entailed. Football was the most important thing in my life, with my social life a close second. Home seemed to be a very distant third. Hanging around with the likes of Jeff Rafferty and Keith Mason was bringing me into contact with a lot of girls that I probably would not otherwise have met.

I remember one weekend going out with the lads and picking up a gorgeous redhead who made it clear she was mine for the night. My wife was away visiting her family so I took her back to my place - I was totally shameless. Sure enough, she stayed the night and left the next morning and I felt sure I had got away with it. That Sunday afternoon my wife came home and asked who had been using her hairbrush. I looked in horror as Sylvia confronted me with the brush, which was filled with long, dark red hairs. Quick as a flash I came up with my excuse. I told her: "One of the lads came round while he was out walking his dog - a red setter - and needed to brush it. I said it would be OK to use your brush." I know she didn't believe me but I stuck to my story for the rest of my married life.

The following Saturday we entertained South Liverpool at our home ground, the Moss Rose. Half an hour before kick-off the heavens opened and it just kept on raining. The conditions were atrocious but it helped us to solve one of life's little mysteries.

Ever since my arrival at Macclesfield Town I had been baffled by the fact that our sponge man had really jet-black hair, despite his advancing years. He insisted it was entirely natural, but this very wet afternoon finally exposed the truth.

Midway through the second half, one of our players went down heavily under a nasty challenge, so our physio leapt into action. Now, he always wore a cap but on this particular afternoon, for some reason, he had left it at home. After giving some treatment to our injured player he returned to the bench, right at the height of the downpour, after getting a real good soaking. His face looked like a zebra crossing, as the heavy rain had brought all the dye out of his hair and sent it cascading down his cheeks and all over his neck!

We won 3-0, but after the game I asked Jimmy to make some enquiries about South Liverpool's number six, a tough-tackling midfield player, and their number nine, a tall, thin centre forward with a real eye for goal. South Liverpool were already hovering around the bottom three so we fancied it may be an opportunity to tempt some of their best players over to Macclesfield.

Jimmy worked fast and by the following day had arranged a Monday night meeting with both of these lads at a pub called the White Lion in Liverpool. The midfield player was called Phil McFarren - the striker was John Aldridge. Aldridge, of course, went on to become one of the greatest centre forwards in the modern game and he is still Britain's top post-war goalscorer with more career goals than even the great Jimmy Greaves. He also gained 69 caps for the Republic of Ireland and helped Liverpool win the League Cup in 1987 and the League title in 1988.

We made offers to both of the lads and McFarren accepted immediately. John Aldridge was keen to sign but told us that he had also arranged to meet with the manager of Newport later that week and he was hopeful of being offered a full-time contract, so asked if he could delay his decision until Friday.

Watching Aldridge against Macclesfield that afternoon, I could tell he had a touch of class and a goalscorer's eye, something my team badly needed.

Little did we know what a fantastic career lay ahead of this likeable young Scouser. In fairness, John kept his word and rang me the following Friday night to tell me that he had signed a two-year deal with Newport, but he thanked me for the generous offer. I wonder if he would have enjoyed quite such a successful career if he had signed for me instead!

When you are fortunate enough to get your hands on a young player like John Aldridge, as we found with Peter Coyne at Ashton, you can often gain a large financial reward for your club further down the line which can sometimes change the entire direction of the football club.

It was well known at the time that Macclesfield had big financial problems, but so did many other non-league clubs. However, after two seasons of up and down results I realised that this was probably the worst time for me to be in this particular job, which had quite a high profile in non-league football. My marriage was completely shot to pieces, while my social life was beginning to take its toll: too many late nights and not enough sleep. It was no surprise when I was called to a board meeting at the ground and told that the football club had decided to dispense with my services.

No matter whether you manage Macclesfield Town or Manchester United, it is hard to accept that you have been sacked for the first time in your career.

On my way home that night, I resolved to sort my domestic life out as quickly as possible and then get my football career back on track.

We signed Peter Coyne from Manchester United - Live on TV!

The original main stand at The Moss Rose.

Me and the Macc Lads.

Macc Town: The smallest changing room in the league - before development!

MACCLESFIELD TOWN F.C.
Price 5pence

1979-80

SUPPORT OUR LOTTERY
M. T. F. C. DEVELOPMENT ASSOCIATION

INSTANT CASH PRIZES

WEEKLY PRIZE £1000

AGENTS WANTED — APPLY CLUB OFFICE PHONE: 24479

Macclesfield matchday programme v Ashton United.

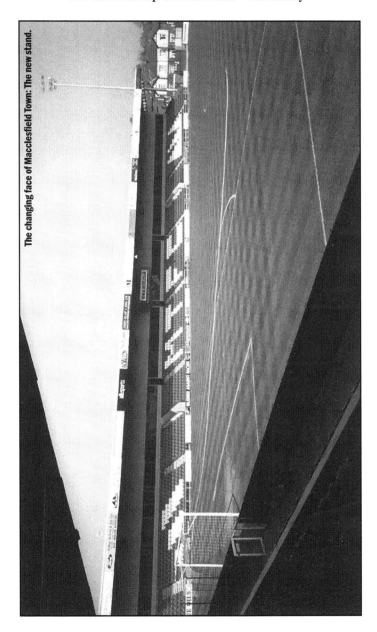

The changing face of Macclesfield Town: The new stand.

Get Those Sheep Off The Pitch! - Phil Staley

4

The best club in the world

Still hurting from my sacking at Macclesfield Town, the time had come for me to join the club I still regard today as the best in the north of England. No, it is not Liverpool, Manchester United, Manchester City, Blackburn Rovers, Everton or Bolton Wanderers. It isn't even Stockport County. It was Bredbury Hall Country Club, a famous nightspot that was heaving with talent every single week.

Every Friday, without fail, my good friend Peter Coughlin and me would go there to see what we could pick up. Peter was very involved with the Communist Party at the time, so we called him "Commy Peter". His marriage was also going slowly down the tubes so every Friday at 7.30pm we would head for Romiley Sauna, stay until eight o'clock, then travel into the centre of Stockport for a couple of hours at the Unity pub before heading for my new club, Bredbury Hall.

For veterans of the night-club scene in Stockport

back in the seventies and eighties, they will remember Bredbury Hall as being riddled with caves, nooks and crannies all over the place. The dance floor was always packed and Peter and I would always head for the Boddingtons Bar, which had a birds eye view of the dance floor, as well as two of the surrounding bars.

We used to buy our drinks and then stand with our backs to the bar, pulling in our stomachs and watching it all happen around us. After last orders had been called, we would generally make a move on anyone who had caught our eye during the evening. We left it late so that if we DID pull, then it wouldn't cost us in drinks because the bars were closing.

One particular Friday we went straight to the Unity because the previous Sunday I had broken my wrist playing in a charity match for BBC Radio Manchester up at Newton Heath, the original home of Manchester United. I told Peter that a sauna would not be a good idea this evening because of the bandage.

But we still followed the rest of our ritual and, after a couple of pints, headed off to Bredbury Hall, but we agreed that we would call it a night early on because my wrist was still pretty sore. Making our way in, we headed for our usual bar, ordered a couple of pints and took up our normal stance, eyes shiftily scanning the room for anything in a skirt. We had just assumed our scouting positions, when Commy Peter noticed a blonde moving very nicely on the dance floor alongside a smaller lady with a neat, curly perm. Pete suggested we split them up and have a dance, but with most of my arm in plaster, dancing was the last thing on my mind. I was also loath to make a move at this early stage, with the bar still being open. I pointed out it could cost us a fortune in Martini Biancos.

But Commy Pete was adamant about dancing with the blonde and marched his six foot four inch frame over to her and asked for the next dance - to my amazement, she accepted, leaving her friend to take a seat just a few yards away.

I noticed she was smoking, which is usually a turn-off for me, but I decided to make a move. To be honest, I felt a bit of a lemon standing there on my own, so I went over and broke the habit of a lifetime: I offered to buy a drink. It turned out to be a stroke of genius. She was called Andrea - we talked for a while, had a dance or two and then I offered to take her home.

There was one snag – that morning in the papers the front pages were dominated by Jack the Ripper, later revealed as Peter Sutcliffe. He was due to strike again and the papers said his next victim would be in Manchester on that very night. With my arm in plaster and somewhat the worse for drink, I didn't look a safe bet to Andrea that evening!

However, we arranged to see each other at a later date, little knowing that she was destined to become the next Mrs Staley. One thing led to another and after a couple of months, we both ended up working at Manchester Airport, which meant we could see even more of each other.

We decided to move into a rented flat together. Nothing in football was ever as hard as the day I packed my cases and left my two sons with my ex-wife. There were more traumas over the next few months, as well, with the various legal proceedings taking their course. The divorce went through leaving Andrea and I free to marry, something I had sworn never to do again.

Football had taken a back seat through all this personal upheaval; I was working for British Airways, while Andrea had a job at Ringway with Hertz car rentals. But we both agreed it might be wise to move out of the area for a while. On the grapevine, I had heard that BA were preparing to offer severance to their existing staff, but the deals were still 16 months away. I also heard that in the coming months, BA were planning to take on temporary staff for the summer season.

Andrea landed one of the temporary posts and I put in for severance for the following year. It meant we could organise our shifts so we worked together for the next twelve months. But in the meantime we applied to join the licensing trade with Bass Northwest - and the application was accepted.

We counted the months down until, in March 1983, we left BA together and took over the tenancy of a pub in Anglesey called The Red Dragon in a little village called Llaingoch. Having spent some time managing in the Welsh League, I thought this would be a good location for us. My team had played many times against Holyhead Town and I thought people would still remember the times at Bethesda. In the back of my mind, I guess I was also hoping that I might be able to re-establish myself in non-league football, as there were frequent openings for experienced managers in the Welsh League.

But there was one small matter to attend to before we could make the move and that was the task of selling our little bungalow that we had bought with the money left over after my divorce. Luckily, after just one month, we had sold up and were ready to start our new lives and careers in the licensing trade. It was probably as close as I would ever get to going into Europe!

It didn't take long for us to settle in and for me to find out about the local football clubs on the island, and it came as no surprise when after just three weeks, I found myself training and coaching the town football team. I wanted to make a big impression on these lads so I really worked them hard. I could always tell when it was hurting them because they stopped speaking English and started swearing about me in Welsh. But that just made me work them even more.

These lads were playing for the love of the game, no money was put in their pockets for turning up each week, they lacked discipline, but they liked a good drink and, if they were really lucky, a fight afterwards, as well. Most of the players I had with me worked on the ferries that make regular runs across to Ireland, usually twice a day. One thing the training achieved was to make them a bit quicker getting off the boat and into their local on the island.

But it was helping them to get better results on the park, as well, and there had been a gradual improvement. Then, out of the blue, I got a phone call from the manager of Bangor City, a certain former Welsh international called John Mahoney. He asked if I would be interested in joining him as first team coach at Farrar Road. Because of my new business commitments, plus having just got married for the second time, I said I would sleep on it and give him an answer the next day - in reality I already knew what the answer would be.

I spoke to Andrea about the request, trying to use the argument that the extra cash would come in handy. I also told her that it would involve just two evenings a week, as well as Saturday afternoon - but Saturday was the big problem. That was always a busy day in the pub, so to pay for additional staff to cover for my absence would instantly wipe out the meagre amount

I had been offered by Bangor.

But once again my ego took over and we got round the problem with a bit of help from a close friend who agreed to help out in the pub on Saturday afternoons, as long as I worked Fridays so her and Andrea could go shopping in Chester. The negotiations had been as tense as David Beckham's contract talks, but the deal was struck - that evening I rang John and accepted the job.

That Thursday night, I set off for Bangor, a trip of around thirty minutes, but I had reckoned without the additional local difficulties. In the winter months, the farmers on Anglesey would move their herds of cattle and flocks of sheep from field to barn and back again. En route I found myself confronted with a herd of about eighty cows being driven from one field to another along a narrow stretch of island road...and I was right in the middle of them.

There was cow shit everywhere and I found myself stranded in the middle of eighty Friesians crapping all over the road - and all over my car. It looked like a camouflaged army vehicle, splattered from front to back. After seventy minutes in the car I finally reached my destination, Farrar Road, smelling like a cowshed. I was greeted my the club chairman, ex Football League ref Gwyn Pierce Owen who saw me and asked if I'd decided to take over a farm instead of a pub. I was grateful when he offered to have my car taken down to the local garage for a clean up while I got on with the training session.

John Mahoney and I hit it off straight away and our work on the training ground soon produced results on matchday, as we took points from my first three games at Bangor City. But already there were two major stumbling blocks. At the time, Bangor City were members of the Northern Premier League, which meant all but one of our away fixtures were played in England. Also, John liked to socialise after every training session and every match. It meant my time away from the pub was proving too long and our business was starting to suffer. After a string of long trips and some marathon drinking sessions, Andrea showed me the yellow card.

It had been a stormy time on the football field for me, too, as I had received two more fines for shouting abuse at the match officials, which meant it was actually costing me money to do the job. After three months I quit, before the yellow card from my wife turned into a red one.

With hindsight, being confined to a pub in Holyhead is not a life I would recommend to anyone and, after just two years in the business, we sold the tenancy and moved back to Poynton, near Stockport, and found new jobs for ourselves.

Within six weeks, I was back in non-league football, this time with a small local club called Grove United who rang me out of the blue and asked if I would help them out. I felt it might be a stepping stone towards re-building a career in the game, despite the lack of any financial reward from the post, so I accepted it. At least it would keep me busy on a Saturday afternoon.

This appointment brought me together with a guy I had a lot of respect for as a player, Tony Keyes. Tony had played at a high level in football during a career taking in Stockport County as well as an appearance at Wembley for Stafford Rangers in an FA Trophy Final. I was delighted when he agreed to join me as player-coach at Grove United. It turned out to be probably the least traumatic post I ever held in football. As money was not involved at all, football became a sport again, rather than a business. But we maintained a level of discipline and trained once a week, while the lads paid their subs and used their own cars to travel to games.

We had a terrific team spirit and that proved a great asset as we had an excellent run in the Saturday Cheshire Amateur Cup and found ourselves in the top three of the league for most of the season. But it was our cup run that caught the local headlines, as well as the attention of some big names in the non-league scene.

After a couple of easy ties we found ourselves up against Heswall in the third round, a team that had won the cup themselves a couple of times before.

They included a couple of players who went on to bigger clubs and we knew it would be a tough fixture. One of their players was a lad called Steve Whitehall, the Ian Rush of amateur football, a striker who scored goals for fun.

The cup tie was played in early December and on the morning of the game the pitch was covered in pools of standing water, so the committee organised a working party to clear the pitch. When I arrived at about 10.30am I joined in. We got out the garden forks, a big brush and a small roller wrapped in a sponge. I bet Sir Alex never went through this.

After two hours of hard graft, and fingers crossed for no more rain, the pitch was still heavy, but playable. We rang Heswall and told them to travel, the ref gave the pitch the thumbs up and the opposition arrived on time: game on!

Inside three minutes, Steve Whitehall had given Heswall the lead, but just before half-time we got our lifeline as a back pass got stuck in the mud allowing Tony "Sniffer" Clarke to steal in ahead of the goalkeeper and score the equaliser. Within eight minutes of the restart, Geoff Kershaw, known as "The Bird", flew down the wing, cut inside and unleashed a shot which thumped into the back of the net. When sub Paul Smith increased our advantage, we knew we had the fitness to hold onto the lead on the mud soaked pitch - we were home, but certainly not dry.

Reaching the fourth round was a tremendous result for a club of our size, considering the team consisted of players paying £3.00 per week for the right to wear the shirt. It was back to the Horse and Jockey in Hazel Grove to celebrate. The only win bonus on offer was pies, peas and a few pints, but the talk now was about Grove United going all the way in this competition.

Sure enough, three more tough ties were successfully negotiated and we reached the final to take on the new favourites for the competition, Higher Bebbington. They were four points clear of Heswall at the top of the West Cheshire League, so we knew it was going to be a ridiculously tough fixture for the lads. But we had reached the final, so there was really nothing for us to lose and I made sure that we would enjoy our trip to Chester.

The final was to be played at Sealand Road, then the home of Chester City, so the committee, me and "Desert Orchid" himself Tony Keyes felt that the players deserved a hotel stopover at the Royal Oak in Hoole, near Chester. I made arrangements for us to train on the Saturday morning at nearby Christleton's ground.

But there was one major risk staying overnight - and that risk came in the shape of Tony Burke. Tony was a fantastic character, but was also famous for his drinking exploits, a real Jekyll and Hyde character after a few pints of ale. He lived life to the full but it was still a major shock to hear he had passed away just before I started writing this book.

We arranged to pick the lads up at the Horse and Jockey the night before the game and drive to Chester at 6pm. I think one or two had probably spent the afternoon in the pub, but I could not really complain. By the time everyone had checked into the hotel near Chester it was 8.30pm and all the lads had agreed to abide by a midnight curfew. Sure enough, all the players returned to their rooms in good time. That left me, the committee and Tony sitting at a table discussing the game with our sponge man, who just happened to be the drummer from the Hollies, Eric Haydock. Eric loved his football, but had a cruel streak - he loved throwing freezing cold water over players who were feigning injury when in fact they had been on the piss the night before.

We were deep in conversation in the bar area, when we noticed the door leading to the players' bedrooms was slightly ajar. Protruding from behind the door was a penis, the size of a baby's arm. It had to be Tony. He had a reputation for being the only player in the league to wear a hammock for a jockstrap. Everyone sitting around the table burst out laughing, which was the worst thing we could have done, because Tony Burke needed little encouragement. Within seconds he was prancing around the bar, completely naked. Eventually he disappeared and we returned to our drinks and our conversation, which included a grovelling apology to the manager of the hotel, who I have to say took it in good spirit.

The following morning, we trained for an hour, had a light lunch and then set off for Sealand Road, knowing we had prepared properly for the big game (with the exception of Tony's antics in the bar). One of the hardest jobs you face as a manager of any side is telling players they are not going to be involved in a big game, and explaining why you have chosen to leave them out. It seems even harder when the players aren't getting paid. To make matters worse, I made a bad decision on this occasion and left the wrong lad out of the side. But to his credit, Dave Goodwin accepted it well.

After the first 45 minutes, I felt we should have been in front, so I opted to bring on sub Paul Smith for Geoff Kershaw for the second half. Our biggest problem had been the right wing where Simon Howarth had been ineffective. During my half-time talk I heard him ask for a paracetamol and I went berserk. I knew he was suffering with a hangover, so I immediately called for another sub to take Simon's place. He wasn't happy, but the decision was made.

After ninety minutes the two sides were still locked at nil-nil, so the final went into extra time, but still no-one managed to break the deadlock. The Cheshire FA decided to hold the replay at my old team's ground,

Macclesfield Town, the following Saturday. What an afternoon it turned out to be. We went a goal in front after just ten minutes before all hell broke loose. Our centre half Nick Heyward went up for a free-kick and as the ball was crossed to the far post he leapt like a salmon out of water and thumped a header into the far corner of the net. The referee signalled a goal, but after the goal celebrations died down we all spotted the linesman on the far side with his flag raised. The officials held a brief confab before the referee decided to change his mind and give the opposition a free kick instead.

At this stage, I lost my head. I charged round to the other side of the pitch to ask the linesman what he was playing at, but he refused to comment. His only words were: "Go away." I stood face to face with him and told him: "Take your flag and shove it up your arse, you cheating bastard!" or words to that effect. Again, he summoned the ref over, they spoke for a moment and then the ref took me to one side and told me to watch the rest of the game from the main stand.

But there was more to come. Bebbington equalised with the last kick of the game forcing the match into extra time once more. During the added time I discovered from a spectator in the stand that the three officials were all from the Wirral and all officiated in the West Cheshire League.

We lost the game in the last minute of extra time,

by which time I was ready to declare a jihad on the officials. I stormed down to challenge the referee as he left the field to ask why our second "goal" had been disallowed. He replied: "That's my business, not yours." I followed him all the way to the dressing room and as he closed the door behind him, I threw it wide open again to continue demanding an explanation.

The unholy triumvirate refused to comment so I picked up their tray of tea and threw it all over them as they huddled in a corner of the compact Moss Rose changing room. I turned and left. Never in my life have I felt so sorry for a bunch of players as I did that day - even now I still insist they were cheated. Four weeks later, despite an appeal, I was banned for three months and fined £150, which really put the icing on the cake at the end of a season which had promised so much.

Me, front row, 2nd right, before a Hollyhead charity match.

Farrar Road - home to Bangor City

Torkington Park - home of Hazel Grove United.

Hair by Gary Bingham - before Grove's big game with Chester.

I pulled up at Bangor covered in cow pats!

The late Gary Burke celebrating Cheshire FA Saturday Cup semi-final win.

Get Those Sheep Off The Pitch! - Phil Staley

5

Banned from the ground

Disciplinary problems apart, it had been one of the most enjoyable and pressure-free seasons I had spent in football. That summer I received a phone call from David Sterling who had recently taken over the Chairmanship of a local non-league side called Droylsden FC. Having spent ten months at the football club, David was finding it tough going and was finding success particularly difficult to come by. Even in that short space of time he had gone through two managers already and had become renowned as a guy who was loath to part with the pennies, never mind the pounds.

As David's reputation preceded him, I was cautious when he gave me the call, but I agreed to meet him the following night. At this meeting, David laid out his masterplan for Droylsden FC and revealed he had kept a close eye on my own progress since returning from Wales. He finally cut to the chase and asked if

I would be interested in taking over as manager for the coming season. Throughout our conversation there were constant references to "tight reins" and "minding the pennies" but he still managed to sell the job to me.

David explained that Droylsden would give me a good opportunity to make my name again in non-league football, even though I admitted my disciplinary record was shocking, to say the least. I knew I would have to watch my mouth in future because it was actually costing me money to manage football clubs. David told me he wanted a brash, extrovert character in charge, so I agreed to give it a go, after agreeing a wage bill, my own terms and bonuses for the following season. There was just one problem - Droylsden FC had only one player left on their books!

Thankfully the player in question, Darren Lyons, was a talented lad, although, like me, he was no stranger to the FA's disciplinary procedures. He would prove to be a player who would provide me with many good times, as well as a string of problems. My faithful sidekick Tony Keyes agreed to come with me as Player/Coach, which doubled the playing staff overnight. Between us we spent the entire close season scouring the lower leagues and signing new players, whilst keeping strictly within the Chairman's tight budget. He refused to spend a penny over his projections, but to be fair to David, the wages were always paid on time.

Putting an entirely new team together from the nether regions of the footballing ladder is a nightmare, but it proved to be an interesting challenge for both of us, while the season I spent with Grove United had been a good grounding for the job in hand. The Mid-Cheshire League I knew was always full of decent players who were capable of making a step up. Bear in mind, these boys had been paying subs for most of their careers, so to be suddenly offered a wage was quite a shock to some of them.

By the start of the new season, the team we had put together at Droylsden consisted of no less than nine players from the Mid-Cheshire League. I snapped up four from a team called Rylands FC, three from my old club Grove United and two from Kidsgrove Athletic. My best signing, though, was a young goalkeeper from Aston Villa - yes, Aston Villa! Gavin Ward had just been released by the Midlands club and, at the time, was struggling to find a league club to take him on. I somehow managed to convince Gavin that Droylsden was the best place for him to reignite his career. I told Gavin that, if he signed and helped me out for a few games, I would make sure he got back into the Football League. He agreed to the deal we were offering and we were able to name a side for our first league fixture of the season.

The pre-season friendlies had gone very well

and we felt quietly confident that the lads would give their all and make a decent fist of the coming campaign. Both Tony and I felt it was important to have strong characters in the dressing room and one of our best assets proved to be Alan Blair, a left back from Warrington, who was a tremendous influence on and off the field. Another was Phil Chadwick, a young player making a name for himself after leaving Rylands FC along with Darren. Both of them were like shit off a blanket, which was giving opposing defences plenty of problems.

Our league form proved to be up and down but we got a great result in the first round of the FA Trophy, beating Fleetwood away from home, but in the end it proved to be a costly victory. Cardiff City had spotted our young keeper Gavin Ward so, true to my word, I agreed to let him go. He was a non-contract player, under the terms of our agreement, so we could not ask for a fee for him. On the open market, he probably would have commanded a five-figure fee...we were presented with six footballs, instead, with Cardiff's grateful thanks.

I had to find an immediate replacement for Gavin, so snapped up the giant Ian Rowbottom from Chadderton. But we needed more cover so I signed two more players with the Chairman's blessing, who stayed with me for several seasons to come. Both were over six feet tall, one a centre half, the other a centre forward, Ray Sidderley and Bernie Hughes.

The next week, the draw was made for the next round of the Trophy - we landed Rossendale United at our home ground, the Butchers Arms. We were in confident mood, despite losing Gavin, because we now had a backbone to the team with Ian, Ray, Bernie and Phil, while Darren was skinning full backs and firing in crosses for the front men.

The day of the cup tie arrived - it was horrible. Outside, it was wetter than the front row of a Barry Manilow concert. It was cold and windy, as well, but we put Rossendale to the sword that afternoon and ran out three-nil winners. But the celebrations didn't last long. On Tuesday night I received a phone call from Roy, the club secretary, to inform me that Rossendale had put in a complaint to the FA, arguing that Darren Lyons had been suspended by the Manchester FA for being sent off playing Sunday football earlier that season. They claimed he should have been serving a suspension at the time of our Trophy fixture.

Darren, who was never one to trouble the hierarchy of MENSA, had failed to mention this fact to anyone at Droylsden because he thought Sunday football had no bearing on his appearances for us. Meanwhile, the FA had ordered an inquiry to be heard at their headquarters in Lancaster Gate the following Wednesday.

In my heart of hearts, I knew it was a waste of

time, but there was a slight chance of having the game replayed, rather than being thrown out of the competition. I headed off to the capital with the Chairman, the Secretary and dozy Darren in tow. We were all smartly dressed for the hearing - except for Darren, of course. He turned up in jeans, a red and yellow shirt, trainers and a Michael Foot-style donkey jacket. He also brought his Sunday League manager along for moral support, big George Rooney. George was known throughout non-league football as the Middleton Destroyer, so we weren't about to argue.

During the train journey to Euston everyone began to rehearse what they might say to the FA Commission. It became clear early on that Darren and George would not be star witnesses. The Chairman, becoming more and more frustrated, disappeared to the restaurant car to get himself some breakfast. When he returned he had a huge stain on the front of his trousers where the waiter had dropped a fried egg into his lap. Things were going from bad to worse, and we hadn't even arrived in London.

As we stepped from the train, the two club officials and I looked as though we had just been to Church. All three of us were dressed in long dark Crombie coats. But that good impression was instantly ruined as Darren appeared wearing his donkey jacket, while George was sporting a particularly hideous TA camouflaged army jacket.

For those of you who have never had the pleasure of a trip to Lancaster Gate, this magnificent building in central London is like the consulting rooms of a top surgeon. A big hall with eight or nine doorways leading off to various corridors and waiting rooms where you sit nervously while the powers that be decide your fate.

We were told that only three of our party would be admitted to the hearing to face the Commission, which came as a relief initially, because it meant we could leave Darren and George outside. But then came the bad news: the FA wanted Darren to be one of the three. In the end, I offered to stay outside with George, which suited me down to the ground. My face was becoming a bit too familiar at Lancaster Gate, so I opted to keep a low profile for once.

As the three of them walked in to face the panel, I couldn't help myself whistling the theme from the Muppet Show. Within fifteen minutes, they were out again, to await the decision of the FA delegation. I would have staked my season's salary on the outcome and, sure enough, it came as no surprise when the verdict was announced. Droylsden were thrown out of the FA Trophy and the club was warned about its future conduct, on top of a fine of £250.

As we headed back up north, the Chairman suggested we should make an appeal, but in the end he agreed with me that it would be a waste of even more time and money. At the mention of money, David swiftly came round to my way of thinking.

As Christmas arrived, we were lying 16th in the league and things were looking a bit bleak for me, but thankfully I had become good friends with the Chairman off the field and it proved a big help during this sticky patch.

By January we had managed to chalk up two wins in a row, thanks to the arrival of two new players, a change of system and a better team spirit in the camp. From the start of the New Year, we never looked back - by March the run had extended to eight wins in a row, despite several postponements due to bad weather. After a dreadful start, we were now starting to fancy our chances of promotion to the Premier Division.

Maximum points from those eight games had lifted us to third place in the table, with a game in hand. Our main rivals for top spot were Eastwood Town and Leek Town, managed by my good friend Neil Baker, now assistant manager to Dario Gradi at Crewe Alexandra. But the season had another sting in its tail for me. Because of our move up the league I had decided to sign another player, who I believed had the quality and experience of non-league football to be able to play in a variety of positions, Paul Moss.

I approached Paul, who was a free agent at the time, and asked if he would join us on a non-contract basis, freeing him up to play for us immediately. He agreed, so our Secretary followed up by visiting Paul at home to acquire his signature. When he arrived, Paul's wife said Paul had gone to hospital to visit a sick relative, but said that she would sign on his behalf.

Foolishly, our Secretary thought this would be OK; Mrs Moss signed the form while he witnessed the paperwork himself before sending it off to the League, without informing anyone at Droylsden FC. That weekend, I was set to give Paul his debut, but when I arrived at the Butchers Arms, the Chairman was in a state of panic. He rushed me to the boardroom - actually a caravan in the corner of the ground with a fan heater - and said: "We are in big trouble with the League."

Eagle-eyed officials had checked Paul's signature against some previous paperwork and discovered that it didn't match, so we were summonsed to attend a meeting the following Tuesday night and ordered to withdraw Paul from the squad. We won the game two-nil, anyway, without Paul, making it nine straight wins. But afterwards there were more heated discussions about the forged signature and we talked long into the night about this latest crisis at the Butchers Arms.

The Chairman had a plan: he asked me to go before the league and say that I had signed the form on Paul's behalf, because of Paul's unscheduled hospital visit. The Chairman's thinking was that if I was found guilty, I would only receive a relatively small fine, but if the club were found to be culpable, then the fine would be a lot bigger. David promised that, whatever size of fine was imposed on me, he would foot the bill. It turned out to be the worst decision I ever made and it was something I regretted for the rest of my career.

We attended the meeting at the Bowden Hotel, which followed a familiar format; a fifteen-minute hearing, where I admitted my "guilt", followed by a delay while the committee reached their verdict. Nearly an hour later we were called back into the room where I would receive my punishment. I was told that this was a very serious offence and, to my amazement, I was charged with bringing the game into disrepute. The committee handed me a three-month ban, fined me £500 and fined the club a further £1000.

Shell-shocked, we left the hotel, with the Chairman muttering under his breath. We headed for the nearest pub so we could get our heads together over a pint. I was dumbstruck, as the words "three-month ban" continued to echo around my head. We were nearing the end of our promotion campaign and now I was being told to stay away from the ground for the rest of the season.

I was not worried about the money, as I trusted David and I knew he would keep his word over the fine I had just received. But to me the three-month suspension was like a life sentence. I was determined not to have the season ruined by this verdict, particularly when I knew I was the innocent party. I set out my plans and told David exactly what I intended to do.

The next day, I put together a long letter, detailing exactly the course of events, as I had decided that coming clean was the only chance I had of reducing my three-month ban. I put pen to paper and appealed to the FA to review my case urgently in the light of my new statement. They wasted no time in replying and set a date for my appeal the following week at the Cresta Court Hotel in Altrincham, which at least saved me from another trip to London! This was the tenth time in my career I had found myself sitting before a disciplinary committee.

After listening to my appeal in detail, the Chairman of the panel asked me to leave the room while they deliberated on my case. Within 25 minutes I was back in front of him. The Chairman of the three-man committee proceeded to criticise my conduct, but accepted that I was acting out of a sense of loyalty to my club. He said they were prepared to show leniency in my case, and would reduce my ban to one month, but ordered that the fines should remain in place. I was also warned about my future conduct - again. I thanked all three members of the panel individually and shook their hands.

I rang David to inform him of the outcome and, at first, he groaned saying he would have preferred to see the fines reduced rather than the suspension. He then suggested taking a small proportion of my wages each week in order to pay off the fine in instalments. After I threatened to quit, he had second thoughts, knowing full well, we had a terrific chance of achieving promotion.

The immediate problem now was getting around the ban which meant I was barred from going into the ground on match days. Training sessions and team meetings were still permitted, but how could I manage my team when I couldn't even enter the stadium? It was then that I made one of the best contacts of my career.

After training the following Thursday night, I was sitting having a drink with my friend Tony Keyes, discussing my dilemma, when I felt a tap on my shoulder. A frail little old lady was standing behind me and she said: "You can use my bedroom, if you like." I paused for a moment - this was the best offer I'd had in ages! But then it dawned on me. The lady, Ethel, lived in one of the old houses which back onto the Butchers Arms, and her back bedroom looked out over the ground through a gap between the stands. Ethel lived alone, her husband had died a couple of years earlier, and she said she would appreciate the company.

But how could I communicate with the team? Then our trainer Syd Thompson hit upon a fantastic idea:

walkie-talkies! That would allow me to talk to Tony on the bench during the games, so I could still relay instructions to the players. We knew it sounded ludicrous, but it might just work. Unfortunately, we couldn't finalise the arrangements because Thursday was bingo night in the social club, so we had to wait for Ethel to finish her game before we could confirm our plans.

When she finally emerged, she offered to take us over to her house so I could check the view from her back bedroom. When we arrived at Ethel's place, the neighbours' curtains were twitching - it was a few years since she had invited three strange men upstairs. The view was perfect, so I arranged to be there on Saturday at 2.45pm.

Meanwhile Tony hit upon another idea to help us out of our predicament. He suggested holding the pre-match team talk at the local Butchers Arms pub, so we arranged with the landlord to use his back room from 1.45pm. The players could then leave for the changing rooms at 2.15pm, whilst I would head off to Ethel's house, clutching my walkie-talkie.

When Saturday came, it was a bitterly cold day and there had been a hard frost all week, but as I headed up to Ethel's front door I could feel the warm glow emanating from her spic and span semi detached. "Good afternoon, Phil," she said. "Everything is ready for you upstairs. Make yourself comfortable and if you need anything just give me a shout."

I walked into her back bedroom and to my amazement she had laid the room out like a mini theatre. She had placed a big red reclining armchair in the prime viewing position. Next to the chair was a lovely side table with four cans of lager perched on top along with a big bag of Quavers. Only Jimmy Saville's chair could rival this one. The heater was switched on and there was a footstool, as well. I thought I had died and gone to heaven.

At five to three, the players took to the field as I settled back with a can of Skol. The walkie-talkies worked a treat and I had a much better view than poor old Tony, sitting below me in the freezing cold dugout. I spent the afternoon glued to the game and the walkie-talkie, shouting phrases such as "get them tighter at the back" or "tell the full backs to push up". I was beginning to wish the FA had left my suspension at the full three months.

By half time we were a goal in front so I gave Tony a few more words of wisdom as he headed off to the dressing rooms. There was a knock on the door and Ethel entered bearing a tray heaving with a huge pot of tea and a selection of fancy biscuits. During the break, Tony propped his walkie-talkie handset up on a ledge in the changing room and turned the volume up full so I could talk directly to the players. It was surreal, as I spouted things like "same again second half, lads!" I wonder if Sven ever gave a team talk over a radio?

The second half continued in much the same vein, until the 82nd minute when Chaddy hit a volley from Darren Lyons' cross straight into the top corner, only for the referee to disallow the goal for offside. I urged Tony to give his handset to the referee so I could abuse him, but Tony stayed put, thankfully.

We protected our lead well and secured another vital three points on an unbelievable afternoon. The next away game was cancelled, leaving us with another two successive home fixtures, which meant another couple of trips to Ethel's back bedroom. On the second of these occasions, Tony was disgusted to find that she had even left me a hot water bottle in the armchair on what was a particularly chilly Wednesday evening.

I completed my month's ban, all the fines were paid up and we were still nicely placed in the top three with four games to go, two at home and two away. We knew we would need two wins and a draw from the remaining fixtures to finish runners-up to Leek Town who, by this time, were too far ahead to catch. Saturday saw us travel to Penrith, lying second from the bottom of the table, and we were expected to gain maximum points once again. But, like all teams fighting for survival, they played out of their skins and we were happy in the end to get a draw, leaving us with a target of two wins from the last three games.

Our next fixture was at home to Matlock Town, and we ran out comfortably 3-0 winners. But I couldn't help glancing up wistfully at Ethel's window during the game. I had already decided to buy her a present for her hospitality over the last few weeks, but still hadn't settled on which gift to buy.

Our next game was at home to champions elect Leek Town. Their manager Neil Baker spoke to me in the run-up to the game to apologise because he could not attend the fixture at the Butchers Arms because of a problem between himself and his Chairman. A Sunday newspaper had run an article headlined "Bonking Baker", after Neil was allegedly heard over an internal telephone having a cosy chat with the Chairman's girlfriend. Neil had been summonsed to the Chairman's house to explain himself but when he got there was confronted by the Chairman wielding a double-barrelled shotgun!

Neil admitted later it was the most frightening moment of his life as the Chairman told Neil he knew what had been going on and ordered him to turn around and run down the driveway "if you want to stay alive." As Neil shot off down the drive, his false teeth chattering, he heard a loud bang and felt a bullet whistle across his shoulder blades, missing the back of his neck by two inches.

Neil wished me well for the midweek fixture and

told me he would be sending a weakened side. I didn't believe him for a minute. However, by 9.30pm that Tuesday evening, 2000 fans packed into the Butchers Arms were celebrating our 4-1 win and our promotion to the Premier Division. It had been the most gut wrenching season in memory with so many highs and lows, but promotion was finally in the bag.

We decided to travel to Lancaster for our final game of the season in fancy dress, all of us, on the train. But I decided to stay away and attend a friend's wedding instead. Having already achieved promotion, it was time to let Tony have his moment of glory and take charge of the side without the walkie-talkie.

Leading Droylsden to promotion - nice shades too!

Droylsden celebrating promotion - with mascot Craig Hanson.

**Droylsden fans
celebrate promotion.**

Droylsden's going up.

Droylsden FC - with Ethel's bedroom in the background.

6

Accrington Stanley - who are they?

There is a saying in life that time waits for no man, and that is certainly true in football. Trying to rest on your laurels or attempting to bask in the warm glow of any kind of success is a fruitless ambition. No sooner have you achieved something, then the pressure is on to achieve something else, even in non-league.

The next target for Droylsden was to make sure we didn't drop straight back down having won promotion, but I knew we were in for a very long, hard season. We managed to keep the nucleus of the squad together and made one or two additions, so I felt confident we could hold our own in a league that consisted of several sides who these days are near the top of the Conference.

But the new campaign got off to a bad start for me before we had even kicked a ball. The Chairman had promised me a pay rise, taking my wages from £35 per week to the princely sum of £45 per week. But when I raised this issue at the next board meeting, the Chairman and the committee went back on their promise and voted to keep my pay packet at the same rate.

The Chairman had his argument ready - he claimed it was because of the fine that had been imposed on me during the previous campaign, which he had paid. But this was the first time I had heard the two matters discussed in tandem, so I left the ground that night feeling pretty annoyed and wondering which way to turn next. The money was not really the issue, because we were hardly talking about life-changing sums, but there was a principle at the heart of this dispute and I felt a genuine grievance.

I spoke to my pal Tony Keyes and we decided to carry on for the time being, and made a good start to the season winning seven points out of a possible twelve, which was quite an achievement in our first season in top flight non-league football.

One of the clubs we did the double over in Division One, and who had pushed us for a promotion spot right up to the last month of the season, was Accrington Stanley, probably the biggest name in non-league football. Most supporters will tell you that one Chairman is more than enough - but Accrington actually had TWO. John Alty and Terry Styring were highly ambitious, however, and their aim was to get Stanley back up to professional status after resigning from the Football League back in 1963.

The call from John Alty came out of the blue. He asked if I would be willing to meet with him and Mr Styring two days later at the Bull's Head pub in Poynton, my home village. Accrington had finished fourth last season, and sixth the season before, so I was surprised to receive a call from them, but quite happy to attend the meeting the following Thursday night.

Now, Thursday nights were normally training nights at Droylsden, so I rang Tony to tell him that I wouldn't be there this week and left him in charge of planning for our home clash with local rivals Stalybridge Celtic that weekend. It was to be our first Tameside derby since winning promotion.

But on that last Thursday of November 1990 I was to have my eyes well and truly opened by the determination and ambition of the two guys from Accrington who told me they wanted a new manager to come in and get them promotion as quickly as possible. They wanted to get up to the Premier Division of the HFS Loans League and believed that, having done it once with Droylsden, Phil Staley could do it again with Accrington Stanley.

They made me an offer there and then which saw my meagre pay packet treble overnight. The wage bill available to me was twice the size of Droylsden's and the final persuasion, as if I needed one, was a brown envelope containing a four-figure sum - a gift for leaving Droylsden FC!

As I left the Bull's Head that night, I was beginning to believe in Father Christmas again. The two gentlemen had made just one proviso - I had to give them a yes or no by midnight on Saturday. That would give me a whole week to prepare for Accrington Stanley's next home fixture.

As soon as I got home, I was on the phone to Tony and asked him how training had gone and made sure there were no absentees for Saturday: no injuries, no illnesses, no weddings! Then I dropped my bombshell and told him I was prepared to drop down a division again - and asked him to join me once more. He didn't seem sure at first, but when I told him I could double his money, he asked: "When do we start?"

I made a call to John Alty to formally accept the offer from Accrington and then sat down to write my letter of resignation to Dave Sterling at Droylsden. It was a difficult thing to do because, until the pay dispute, Dave and I had become pretty close friends off the field, so I decided to hand the letter to him after the final whistle on Saturday. In the letter, I didn't tell him about the financial rewards on offer at Accrington Stanley, but I did stress our disappointment at the lack of reward for our achievements in winning promotion.

A four-figure gate watched our game against

Stalybridge on the Saturday, but I have to admit it was difficult to focus fully on the fixture. The players seemed to sense that something was in the air and the atmosphere was all wrong that day. It certainly affected their performance as they slumped to a 2-1 defeat, although Stalybridge were an excellent side who went on to win the title that season and gained promotion to the Conference.

After the final whistle, we sat down with the squad and told them of our plans to join Accrington. We thanked them all for their efforts over the last couple of seasons before heading for the boardroom, the now-familiar caravan in one corner of the ground. Tony and I knocked on the door and stepped inside to meet the committee, who were all eating buns and drinking tea - we could have been at Filey Holiday Camp.

But the digs started as soon as we walked up the little metal steps: "We need a new striker," said one. "The back four were a bit slow today," said another. All these remarks made it easier to hand over the letters of resignation, which prompted a much worse level of abuse. "You shithouse pair of gold-digging wankers," was one of the best. They offered no words of thanks, no good wishes, not even a sticky bun. Tony and I turned and walked out and, I have to say, we both knew then that we had done the right thing.

Joining Accrington in the winter of 1990, I began to

realise what a household name the club was all over the world. Wherever I have travelled, people have always heard of Accrington Stanley. We quickly began to build our side to win promotion to the Premier Division. My first signing became one of my most significant as we forked out £1000 to Rossendale United for the services of striker Paul Beck.

I then went back to Droylsden to sign a player who had been very loyal to me over the years, Bernie Hughes. Bernie was a six-foot centre forward but had a natural athleticism and was very good on the floor. We converted him to a central midfield player with great effect.

Tony Keyes wanted to concentrate on coaching at Accrington, so I decided to appoint someone else as my assistant manager so I approached the former South Liverpool centre half John Benden to come and work with me. John had fantastic connections on Merseyside and he immediately brought four players with him, so we set our stall out for a promotion campaign.

By the end of the season we had guided Stanley up to fourth place in the HFS Loans League, which would not normally be good enough. But in 1991, South Liverpool resigned from the Premier Division, which opened up a third automatic promotion place. The team immediately above us, Worksop Town, were told their ground was not up to the required standard and they were unable to upgrade within the time limit allowed. Stanley's promotion to the Premier Division, albeit in fortunate circumstances, was confirmed. The cries of "Stanley are back!" rang around Hindburn as Accrington took their place in the top flight.

It gave the whole region a big lift, and gates went up as well, but our first season in the Premier Division proved a difficult one as we tried to steady the ship, and I had several rows with John Benden over who should be playing in the first team. It called for ruthless measures and I held long discussions with Tony over our future plans.

We decided to give the squad a facelift and released eight first team players, as well as parting company with John. Tony agreed to take on the role of assistant manager once more and we brought in several quality players to freshen up the squad. They included Steve Lampkin, Martin Clark, Charlie Cooper, Eddie Johnson, Stuart Owen, Terry Williams, Paul Burns, Mike Lutkevitch, Jim McCluskie and Ashley Collins, who was a dead ringer for Phil Collins! We also re-signed Paul Beck, Bernie Hughes and three other players in the existing side.

But as we had found at Macclesfield, money was a major problem - or rather the lack of it. In July 1992, with their first Premier Division season behind them, Accrington Stanley appealed via the local media for more support in their fundraising efforts. Chairman

John Alty told the local paper: "The present squad looks to be an extremely strong one. It is, however, essential that our income is increased substantially if we are to fund the payments to these quality players which we possess."

The appeal worked. The club gradually alleviated its most pressing debts as money started to trickle into the football club as the fans gave their backing to the team in 1992/93. And they were rewarded instantly, as the team was about to embark on a thrilling run in the FA Cup that caught the imagination of the whole town.

Brian Clough once famously wrote a book containing a chapter detailing the average Chairman's knowledge of the game of football - the chapter was completely blank. But our Chairman Mr John Alty must have known a thing or two about talent, because it was around this time that he invited me to become a Director of Accrington Stanley! He said it was a sign of the club's appreciation for my efforts. I couldn't believe it, but I didn't hesitate, of course, and snatched the guy's hand off.

By this time, Mr Alty had split with Mr Styring after the pair had a disagreement of some kind, which caused Mr Styring to resign from the Board of Directors. As a result, I now found myself in the bizarre position of having my feet very comfortably under the manager's table as well as the board room table. I started to contemplate the day when I might have to cast my vote to sack myself as team manager!

As I was now a paid Director, I decided to earn my keep by going out into the town to actively seek some sponsorship for the club. The company I worked for full-time had already agreed to back the club by sponsoring a match, plus a few other fundraising events, but I felt I wanted to justify my new status at the Crown Ground off the field by bringing in more revenue.

On the field, after losing our opening fixture and drawing the next, we lost our two registered goalkeepers in two consecutive games through injury and I was left with just three days to find a replacement. I have to say, I played a blinder! I signed a new keeper called Paul Collings who took Stanley onto another level. Paul had been an England Schoolboy International and he quickly displayed his qualities with a stunning penalty save in only his second game for me at home to Leek Town. The Stanley defence clearly grew in confidence with a keeper of Collings's quality behind them and he went on to play 27 games for them, finishing up on the losing side on just three occasions.

On September the 26th 1992 Accrington Stanley against Bradford Park Avenue in the second qualifying round of the FA Cup was billed as a battle between two former football league clubs. A brace from Paul

Beck saw Stanley comfortably through to the third qualifying round and far tougher opposition. We were drawn away to Conference club Stalybridge, but we outclassed them from start to finish and thoroughly deserved our 2-1 victory.

This result earned Stanley a home tie against Northern League side Northallerton Town in the fourth and final qualifying round and, by this time, the town was buzzing with Cup fever. Well over a thousand fans saw us defeat Northallerton 3-1 in an absorbing game.

It was time to hit the sponsors as we entered the first round proper of the world's greatest domestic cup competition. Thanks to radio and TV exposure we were able to attract masses of interest from commercial outfits such as Holland's Pies who decided to double their sponsorship outlay. Gibson's Sportswear backed us by providing a new strip for the big occasion. We even called a press conference outside their shop in the middle of town and had a photocall with the new kit and dozens of meat pies.

Naturally we were hoping to land a league club in the first round, but we landed a home tie against Conference outfit Gateshead, and it turned out to be a memorable occasion in front of the TV cameras and a sell-out crowd of 2270. At one point a surge from the crowd actually buckled part of the railings behind the goal, but thankfully no one was injured.

A seventh minute strike from Paul Beck (who else?) gave us the ideal start in the game but the visitors equalised just two minutes later and we were hanging on a bit up until half-time. Within six minutes of the restart, Beck struck again to put us 2-1 in front and went on to put the game beyond Gateshead's reach by completing his hat trick. The Conference side did pull a goal back, but we ran out 3-2 winners.

The celebrations were unprecedented - since the club's reformation in 1968, this was easily the furthest they had gone in the competition and the media spotlight was well and truly on Accrington Stanley. The following week, the Marketing Manager from Holland's Pies organised a photocall with all the team, the directors, Tony and myself. I had to hold a huge tray full of meat pies and steak puddings while the players pretended to eat them.

By the end, we were left with a tray full of half-eaten and nibbled pies. I asked the Marketing Secretary: "What happens to these pies now?" She said: "We'll throw them away." I told her to put them into their original boxes and the lads could take them home for tea. As for me, I got a whole box of pies to myself, most of them with bits missing, but I have to admit I took them home and stuck them straight in the freezer. My wife found out and threw them all away - what a waste!

The following Monday lunchtime I sat with my

ears glued to the radio as the draw was made for the second round of the FA Cup. I can still remember the moment as the draw was made live on air. Our reward for beating Gateshead: a home tie against Crewe Alexandra. Not surprisingly, the profile of the club was about to get even bigger and Paul Beck's phone was ringing day and night with requests for pictures and interviews. The highlights of our win over Gateshead had been shown on Match of the Day, a first for Accrington Stanley who had never entertained BBC Television cameras before that day.

But the draw against Crewe had thrown up a raft of logistical problems. Stanley could only offer a tiny number of tickets to away supporters because of the limitations of the ground, so the decision was taken to switch the tie to Ewood Park, the home of Blackburn Rovers. This would allow Stanley to maximise the income from the tie, but it was a tough decision as it meant taking our biggest game for thirty years away from the town.

It was around this time that the Milk Marketing Board suddenly became interested again in Stanley's achievements and contacted us to request a team photograph. I am sure you can recall the TV ad with the young Liverpool supporter saying to his mate: "If you don't drink your milk, you'll only be good enough to play for Accrington Stanley!" The young star of the advert, who was aged ten by this time, came along to the ground and had his picture taken with the lads.

The players picked him up and suspended him head first over a dozen crates of milk, and one of them was given a cartoon speech bubble on the final picture which said: "If you don't drink your milk, you'll only be good enough to play for Liverpool!"

News of Stanley's achievements had reached far and wide. We heard that an Accrington Stanley supporters club had been formed in Norway - and their Chairman and Secretary were coming over to watch the game at Ewood Park. To my knowledge, the Norway branch is still going strong and they have been over a few times since the cup-tie with Crewe.

The big weekend was approaching and the media were all over the place. To the club's credit, they wanted to prepare properly for this game so a schedule was mapped out for the run-up to the fixture. We arranged to meet at midday on the Friday before the game at the Crown Ground and do an hour's light training, going through a few set pieces and so on. After that, a light lunch in the club house before the players were handed their brand new track suits, white polo shirts, socks and kit bag, donated by Mike Gibson from Gibson's Sportswear in the town.

We then had a couple more TV interviews to get out of the way, before setting off for a local hotel. We decided to stay at the Georgian House Hotel in Blackrod, along with the directors and main sponsors.

To complete a very professional job, we even booked a luxury coach with the team's name festooned across the front. Even 24 hours before kick-off, over a hundred Stanley supporters were there at the ground to wave us off - it was a moment I shall never forget. Even as we pulled away down the main road, I could still hear the cheers and it made the hair stand up on the back of my neck.

We arrived at the hotel an hour later; the lads paired off to check into their rooms while the staff made us feel really welcome. After dinner at 7.30pm, we had a team meeting in the conference room of the hotel and watched a video of Crewe's game against York for the next ninety minutes. The lads went to bed at about ten o'clock but I don't think many of them slept for long.

During the night, the Milk Marketing Board returned, this time to drop off another 16 crates for a photocall the next morning. It must have been one hell of a milk float! For some reason, someone had piled the crates up right outside my room so when I walked out in the morning I crashed headfirst into a wall of white cartons. I had to ring the porters to ask them to move them so I could get out of my room. I think it was two of the squad players who put them there, but no one ever admitted to it.

At 12.30 we met in the lobby to board the coach for our trip to Ewood Park. As we crossed the M61, our driver was stopped by a police motorcyclist who said that he and his colleague would escort us into Blackburn. I missed most of this conversation because Tina Turner's Simply The Best was playing at full blast further down the coach.

As we finally pulled up at the Players' Entrance, we were amazed to see around 500 Stanley fans all gathering around the bus to wish us well and this is a moment that will also stay with me forever. To see the hope, the expectation, the anticipation and the excitement in the eyes of these supporters was absolutely incredible, and anyone who has supported a non-league side can relate to moments like this.

Everything had gone like clockwork, everything had gone to plan, until the game kicked off. We lost 6-1. Crewe took virtually every chance they had. We just couldn't get out of our own half, but despite this, the crowd of 10,801 still gave us a standing ovation as we left the field. Like all managers, you look back on games and wonder if you could have done anything different, and I know that I made a mistake in not playing with a sweeper. All Crewe's goals came through the heart of our defence because the pace of their strikers was just too much for us. Tony Naylor tied Stuart Owen in knots for ninety minutes.

But Crewe had a tremendous team out that day, including Northern Ireland international Neil Lennon, who has since played in the English and

Scottish Premier Leagues with Leicester City and Celtic. And Neil only made the bench that afternoon. Still, this had been our Cup Final, and we had thoroughly enjoyed the experience. And it was weeks before any of us had to buy any pies or milk again.

I taped Match of the Day that night and the next morning I bought every single national newspaper to read the match reports. I still remember reading Bryan Cooney's excellent summary of the game. This particular journalist regularly interviewed surly Scotsman Kenny Dalglish at Ewood Park, as he was then in charge of Blackburn Rovers. This time, I think my post-match press conference came as a breath of fresh air to him.

He wrote: "The absent Dalglish was given a lesson in the art of public speaking by a man who had seen his team hit by a goals avalanche. No one should forget Phil Staley – least of all Kenny Dalglish." I have kept the cutting to this day and it is one of my most treasured memories.

A few weeks after the game, Crewe were in touch with me again as they handed over £10,000 for Martin Clarke. But the rest of our season was always going to be an anti-climax after the FA Cup experience and, sure enough, results in the league were up and down. Thankfully, there was more excitement to come in the close season.

Our Norwegian supporters club invited Paul Beck

and myself to go and visit them for five days, staying with their Chairman Thorkild Gundersen and his Secretary Lars Pieter. The trip would take in a six-a-side competition, which was held every year in Oslo, between various Norwegian supporters clubs. The winning team would receive their trophy from the former Norwegian international Aage Hareide at the Ullaval Stadium during half time at the Norway vs. England World Cup qualifier.

I was asked by Thorkild to manage his team, which would include Paul Beck, of course. We were the only team representing a non-league club, but we caused a huge upset. On our way to the final we beat Ipswich Town, West Ham, Wolves and Leeds, managed by Peter Lorimer. In the final we beat Liverpool 2-0 to take the trophy to cap a tremendous season for Accrington Stanley. It was an incredible moment to walk out in front of 22,000 people in Oslo to receive the trophy on behalf of the Accrington Stanley Supporters Club (Norway Branch)!

Now, I didn't speak a word of Norwegian, but above all the noise I could still make out a section of the crowd singing "Stanley Are Back!" It was a group of England fans from Clayton le Moors. The following day, the Manchester Evening News remarked that it was the only good thing to happen to an English side that night - Graham Taylor's England lost 2-0.

We began the new season with one or two notable

absentees having lost some of our best performers during the summer. Consequently, it quickly became apparent that we were not going to reach the heights of the previous campaign. After a row with the board, caused partly by our poor run of form, I left the Crown Ground just days before a crucial FA Cup 4th qualifying round tie at Conference side Altrincham. It is still a decision I regret to this day and I am sorry I ever fell out with the Chairman. I was on my way out of a club that I had lived, slept, eaten and loved for two and a half years.

SPEAKEASY STALEY

Accrington 1 Crewe 6

UP at Ewood Park, at least once a fortnight, they observe a series of one-minute silences.

These form a vital part of Kenny Dalglish's press conferences. It seems that Dalglish, far from the lights of Liverpool, is still doing for PR what Norman Lamont has done for home accountancy.

Yet the manager who emerged from the home dressing room on Saturday was a revelation.

No suspicious looks, no embarrassing silences, no verbal shorthand.

The absent Dalglish was given a lesson in the art of public speaking by a man who had seen his team hit by a goals avalanche.

BRYAN COONEY on the FA Cup trail

Accrington boss Phil Staley insisted: "There's been no despair in our dressing room. They've had pies, champagne and milk, and they're happy.

"No wonder. Three months ago we had immediate creditors for £10,000 knocking on the door. We were thinking we'd have to sell half the lads who played today. But that debt has been cleared. There's no one knocking on our door now ... we haven't anyone coming to close us down. This Cup run has saved us, without doubt."

It was, of course, a terrible injustice that Stanley surrendered six. They forced 11 corners to Crewe's one, lacking only that clinical finish.

Staley, while acknowledging the injustice of it all, was more concerned by his supporters.

"What about those fans, eh? Magnificent!

"We're reviving and reliving our past. That's why all those fans came today. They know what we want to achieve."

Accrington, the club that died 30 years ago, are back in business.

And no one should forget Phil Staley — least of all Kenny Dalglish.

Fergie eat your heart out! I'm manager of the month.

Drink your milk and play for Accrington.

147

Teaching Norway goalkeeper Erik Thorstvedt a thing or two!

Champions! Receiving our trophy in front of 22,000 fans in Norway.

Me and Don Howe in Norway.

Me and my daughter Lauren Kate.

Paul Beck, me and the Chairman of the Accrington Stanley Supporters Club (Norway branch) Thorkild Gunderson.

7

The Fisherman's Friend

November 23rd 1992 has to go down as the saddest day in my non-league management career; parting company with a famous name like Accrington Stanley was hard to swallow, particularly on the eve of their FA Cup-tie against Altrincham.

One of the biggest regrets was leaving behind a very strong squad of players and, as any manager will tell you, you start to wonder what they might achieve in your absence. But life goes on and, with Christmas on the horizon, I kept myself busy to distract myself from what had gone before. My plan was to stay out of football for a few months, to let the dust settle, before making a firm decision on the future.

Ironically, it came as quite a relief to suddenly find I wasn't involved over the hectic two-week holiday period. I certainly didn't miss ringing players up, arranging transport for them, checking on their health - and finding out who'd been overdoing the sherry. But I must admit, even now, I still check their results every week in the paper, which at the time was probably the worst thing to do.

But with Christmas and the New Year parties out of the way, I found myself itching to get back involved in football again. Then, totally out of the blue, I received a phone call from a guy called Stuart Kay, the chairman of Fleetwood FC. Stuart explained that the football club, which he had just taken over, was in a bit of a mess.

The club had been issued with a winding up order after the exit of the previous chairman and Stuart had come in to pick up the pieces. Little did I know what was in store - I was heading for one of the worst relationships between a manager and chairman in the history of non-league football. Mr Kay promised me the world, but in reality the club's bank account contained tuppence-ha'penny and a bag of marbles. I always say to aspiring young managers now - get everything in writing before you commit yourself in non-league.

Mr Kay told me his plans for Fleetwood, but even then I was struggling to get my head around his wild ambitions. They were bottom of the Premier Division, twelve points adrift and sinking faster than shares in a dot.com company. He felt I was the man to keep them up. In truth, even Viagra wouldn't keep this lot up. But I didn't know much about the football club or the town, to be quite truthful. All I knew was that it had a good reputation for fish and chips and was the global headquarters for the cough sweets, Fisherman's Friends.

But being out of football at the time, I decided to give it a go. This time I decided not to use the old Liverpool connections and contacted a pal of mine called Harry Dunn, who was also out of work at the time, and I asked him to become my assistant. Harry lived in Bishop Auckland and had excellent contacts in the Northeast. I agreed a salary with Harry and we set about getting a side together for our first fixture away to Frickley the following Saturday, at their coal field of a stadium.

Situated in between two enormous mountains of slack and coal dust, going to Frickley is never a pleasurable experience. To make matters worse, their team had got off to a decent start in the league and, by New Year, found themselves in sixth position. As for me, I was taking over a side that had scored just twelve goals and conceded 53 before the snow had even cleared from the ground. You can imagine the task that lay ahead.

We arranged to meet the players on the Thursday night before the game, bring in any new staff we needed and sort out our game plan for Frickley. In such dire straits I used a very simple bit of logic: a good, big player is going to be better than a good, little player. We set out to organise the backbone of the team bringing in a goalkeeper, a centre-half and a central midfielder to give us the building blocks, at least. Just one proviso - they had to be big!

With just these three additions, we met the full squad for training two days before our daunting trip to the coal heaps of South Yorkshire. To my surprise, Harry arrived with a fullback in tow from Sunderland who fancied having a go. I didn't have a clue what he was like, but that's non-league for you! So we started to discuss our game plan with the team - elsewhere, the chairman was meeting a couple of local businessmen who he was trying to persuade to get involved with the club.

But behind the scenes there were major problems, which leapt to the surface almost immediately. We had a coach booked for our first game and the club secretary gave me a list of the various pick-up points for the players en route. It all seemed fairly well organised. Then Dick the kitman approached me and told me the strip the players were due to wear on Saturday was in tatters. Two pairs of socks were a completely different colour to the others and one of the shirts didn't have a number on it.

I said I would have a word with the chairman about the situation, but I knew there was no chance of new equipment being purchased ahead of the game. New kit costs money and so far Mr Kay seemed to be hanging onto his. But he did come up with one idea - he suggested using a thick marker pen to replace the missing number. At this point, I began to have serious misgivings about my latest career move.

But the beauty of non-league football is that you can always expect the unexpected. Amidst all the concerns over the players' strip for the weekend, Dick returned to ask me if I fancied a couple of fresh kippers to take home after the game. I thought this was a nice gesture having just met the guy and gratefully accepted the offer.

Let me try to describe the layout at Highbury Road - that was the name of the ground and it was the only thing we had in common with a club like Arsenal. The changing rooms were tiny and the walls were lined with sheets of hardboard which someone had started to paint but never got round to completing. In the corner was a small table holding a tea tray with a dozen big mugs and a huge steel teapot for halftime.

At the apex of the stand was the manager's office, which was about the size of the hutch occupied by my daughter's rabbit back home. After banging my head a few times, I realised this wasn't the best place to sit and chat to players about contracts or team affairs.

But this was Fleetwood's home and this was where we arranged to collect the locally based players on the following Saturday. The coach and the players arrived on time and the coach set off to our first meeting point

- Birch Services on the M62, where I would also join the travelling party. With only three Fleetwood lads in the side, there were twelve of us waiting at Birch, which was used as a pick-up point by a number of football teams in the Northwest.

We stood and watched as several beautiful executive coaches came and went through the services until one of the lads suddenly shouted: "Here's our bus!" My jaw hit the ground as I watched this ancient relic pull up in front of us. It looked like something out of the Beaulieu Motor Museum. One of the wipers was missing, various panels were hanging off while others were clinging onto the frame of the vehicle thanks to a combination of rust and industrial tape. Smoke was billowing from the back of it as it limped apologetically up the slip road before grinding to a halt in front of us.

All you could hear, once the rattling of the engine subsided, were howls of laughter from the assembled players awaiting their carriage to Frickley. The players, who had been totally focussed on the fixture, had now forgotten all about it as they took in the sight of this hideous charabanc.

I have to say I tried to tread very lightly as I climbed on board with the lads, fearing that one misplaced foot could see me disappear through the floor of this prehistoric conveyance. That was when the smell hit me. The stale aroma of musty body odour hung in the air as I searched the coach for anything that resembled a clean seat. I also knew that Dick had kept his word about the kippers - I could smell them.

As we set off for Frickley I remember seeing one of the lads cross himself and offer a prayer in the hope that we would arrive in one piece. The lads took it in good spirit, though, and, although professionalism was non-existent at Fleetwood, you couldn't fault the spirit, and the journey passed mercifully quickly. But I can still remember the Frickley supporters having a whale of a time when they saw us pull up outside their ground. One of them offered to help us push the coach home after the game.

Red-faced, we trooped past the Frickley directors as they struggled to stifle their laughter and arrived at the tiny dressing rooms. Frickley must be the only club in the country that has a roaring fire in the changing rooms, as they make sure they put all that spare coal to good use. Unfortunately smokeless fuels were a new idea in those days, so we were met with a wall of thick smoke which blew everywhere as soon as we opened the door. Take it from me, this is definitely not the San Siro.

The kit was brought into our smoke-logged dressing room and Dick started to hang it out on the pegs. I watched as the lads changed into shorts and socks that were tattered and torn or had holes in them. I gave my team talk before stepping aside to let Harry take the players through a few set pieces. All the while, the coal snapped and crackled away in the fire making it feel like a holiday cabin in the Alps.

Frickley were lying sixth in the league and we knew what a tall order lay in front of us, but the lads went out and gave it everything, returning at half time leading by one goal to nil. During the first half, more coal had been put on the fire and a pot of tea was stewing on top of the grate when the players returned to the dressing room at the break. All we needed were a few slices of bread, and we could have had tea and toast.

Into the second half and we defended well until the last five minutes of the game when Frickley equalised with a stunning goal which gave our ex-Burnley keeper Chris Pearce no chance. The lads were visibly tiring but they stayed on their toes and hung on to secure a good point away from home, the first the club had taken for several weeks. You would think we had won the World Cup - everyone connected with Fleetwood wanted to come into the dressing room. Every time the door opened the smoke blew all over the place, but we didn't care. It was a great result and even Frickley's manager came in to congratulate us. It was Ronnie Glavin, the ex-Barnsley player who went on to manage Emley with great success.

After accepting a little bit of hospitality - and putting out the fire - we set off again for Birch Services, with the coach now full of beer and crisps and, of course, the stench of the kippers. During the journey, Dick the kitman came up to me and said that if I was to take a cool box to our home fixture the following week, he could fill it with all different types of fish for me to take home. I said I'd get hold of one and proceeded to enjoy the rest of the trip home.

The Chairman spoke about the "one hundred percent improvement" he had witnessed that afternoon and started discussing the possibility of putting the new management team on contract. I felt this was a little premature, plus Harry wasn't with us, as he had travelled directly back to Bishop Auckland in his car (lucky bastard). I told the chairman we would prefer to wait a few weeks to see how things panned out. This turned out to be a very wise move because, the next day, I received a phone call from a representative of Gainsborough Trinity Football Club. He asked if Harry and I would be willing to attend an interview for the vacant management positions at their club.

Harry and I decided that, out of courtesy, we would take up the offer and speak to Gainsborough, one of the founder members of the Northern Premier League. After a cross-country journey, which took almost three hours through Sparrowpit, Baslow, Chesterfield and Worksop, I finally arrived at the ground and met Harry. I must have been mad to even contemplate making this journey twice a week for training and once a week for matches.

However, we entered the ground for an interview with the board of directors, some of whom seemed to think they were in charge of Sporting Lisbon, rather than little Gainsborough. The Chairman gave us a history lesson on the club before outlining his plans for the future. To be honest, we were quite impressed and both agreed that the club appeared to have a bright future. But then, the Club's Financial Director took over, a certain Mr Smith, who I later dubbed The Rottweiler.

Bearing in mind that they had invited us, his attitude surprised me as he began to ask questions about my disciplinary record. The President of Gainsborough Trinity was Ken Marsden, who was also the Chairman of the League, and he had seen me many times before during disciplinary hearings. But Smith went on, and on, and on - he also wanted a financial plan from the pair of us, down to the last penny.

I was just about to get up and leave when the Club Secretary, a gentleman called Frank Nicholson, decided to intervene. He offered us the job there and then. I said we would give an answer the following night. Harry and I agreed the travelling would be a nightmare, and so would Mr Smith, so we decided to stay put at Fleetwood, but use the offer from Gainsborough as a bargaining chip at a later stage, if necessary.

Fleetwood Chairman Mr Kay knew about the

interview and rang me later that night on my mobile to find out what the outcome had been. I told him we had some concerns about the situation at Fleetwood but, if he could help us sort them out, we would be willing to stay until the end of the season, at least. In all honesty, I could never envisage taking the Gainsborough job because of the travelling, whilst Fleetwood had an added bonus: all that fresh fish which I could sell every week!

I rang Frank Nicholson and thanked him for the interview but told him we had decided to stay with Fleetwood. He said: "I don't blame you," and went on to apologise for his belligerent Financial Director. And, for now, I had bigger fish to fry - literally. I set about getting hold of three new cool boxes to take with me to training on Thursday night.

When I arrived at Fleetwood for our second training session, the fog had rolled in from the sea and descended to shroud our pitch in a dense mist. After a couple of minute's deliberation, Harry decided he would use just one end of the ground instead and rehearse set pieces with the players. I disappeared to work on a few set pieces of my own. I knew the chairman was coming to meet me at 9pm so I got Dick the kitman - and now the fishman - to come to my car and collect my three spanking brand new cool boxes ready for Saturday's home clash with Marine.

Saturday arrived, with Marine FC sitting on top of

the league and contemplating another three points. But we made them work for it, eventually losing by the odd goal in a five-goal thriller. Despite the defeat, my bonus was there waiting for me after the final whistle: three cool boxes packed to the top with beautiful fresh fish pulled from the Irish Sea that very morning.

After the game I drove home, got changed and collected my wife Andrea. We set off for our local pub in Poynton, the Bull's Head, collecting a couple of friends on the way. In the boot were the three cool boxes, and dozens of plastic bags. I had kept Andrea in the dark so far about my plan to make a few bob by selling the fish in the pub, but as soon as she got in the car she got a rough idea: "What's that smell?" she cried. I said: "Don't worry, some of the lads had fish and chips after the game and ate them in the back of the car."

After a couple of pints, I left the pub and returned to the car. I had already begun my "pre-match preparations" by creating a typed sheet, which I pinned up inside the pub, and within ten minutes I had my first sale, and there was more to follow. Within the next half an hour I had completely sold out of kippers, cod, plaice, crab sticks, everything. I had made my bonus and a good night was had by all. I also made sure that everyone knew there would be more to follow in the coming weeks.

Over the next few games we picked up the odd point here and there, but not as many as we had expected. The problem now was that it was getting a bit tight at the bottom of the league and the bottom three were closing in. Then we suffered a double blow. We lost our next crucial fixture one-nil at home conceding in the 89th minute, but worse was to come: the landlord of my local banned me from selling fish in his car park. Apparently the customers were complaining about the constant fishy smell every Saturday night. To be honest, it was a blessing in disguise, because my car was in a terrible state. The stale odour of fish hung inside the car and I decided it was time to quit my career as a part-time fishmonger for good.

It was now looking as though our chances of survival in the Premier Division were slim and many of the promises we had been given when we joined the club were not forthcoming. The chairman was getting that sinking feeling and, in typical style, decided it was time to take swift financial action. The first thing chairmen always do in this situation is to slash the wage bill. As half of our wages were going to Harry and the players he brought down from the north east, Mr Kay decided it would be simplest to sever all links with Harry and play four local lads for the remainder of the season instead.

This is where I made a major management mistake. I had always been advised to pay lip service to a chairman and just agree with everything they do, or face the consequences. So I agreed to go along with his plan, instead of telling him to shove his football club up his arse, as I should have done. In hindsight, I would say to any management duo, if you come as a team, leave as a team, because I have regretted this decision for the rest of my life. I told Harry that the chairman and I felt it would be better for the financial future of the club if we parted company now, instead of at the end of the season. And so, our partnership ended, but there was even more trauma to come before the season drew to a close.

The chairman, who had started to show his true colours in recent weeks, called a meeting to take stock of the rest of the campaign and look at my plans for the following season. It was obvious now that relegation was imminent as our form was on such a downward spiral and I had no resources to make any changes. We agreed that now was the time to set out our stall for the following term.

The following Saturday evening, with just four games left, Andrea and I met the former Altrincham right back Stan Allen and his partner Lynn. Stan was out of work at the time but Lynn was urging him to get back into football so I asked Stan to join me at Fleetwood Town with a view to getting promotion next season at the first time of asking. I felt Stan's know-how would give me the opportunity to get things ready for pre-season.

Stan agreed to join me and the chairman gave us the go ahead. We finished the season second from bottom, five points adrift, as expected. But imagine my horror when, just a week after the final ball had been kicked, the chairman told me that my services would no longer be required at Fleetwood Town. I rang Stan to tell him what had happened and told him that I felt the chairman was lower than a snake's belly. Stan seemed to take this disappointing news with considerable ease, and I explained that I had no idea who the chairman had lined up to replace us.

The following Tuesday night, I opened up my copy of the Manchester Evening News and was horrified to read that Stan Allen had been appointed manager of Fleetwood Town. I later found out from the Club Secretary that this decision had been taken a whole week before I was told about my dismissal. Neither Stan nor the Chairman had the decency to tell me sooner. It was a harsh lesson, but it taught me never to trust anyone in non-league football - it was certainly not an easy way to lose a friend.

Still, the chapter does have a silver lining. I had to collect a few things from the ground so I arranged with kitman Dick to meet him outside the ground the following Saturday afternoon so he could hand over my personal belongings. He told me he would have a special selection of freshly caught fish for me as a parting gift. Having a lot of respect for this kind, good-hearted old gentleman, I handed him some money and headed for home, the boot starting to stink again already.

My son Steven, who had travelled with me, thought it would be a good idea to get rid of our haul as soon as possible and buy a deodorising spray so we could disguise the smell before Andrea got wind of it - literally! It was late May by this time and people were starting to enjoy day trips to Blackpool and the Lakes again after the winter break. We decided to pull into a motorway service station for a quick drink and bumped into four old friends from my Accrington Stanley days.

After a brief chat, I asked them if they fancied any fresh fish to take home, which I would sell at a very good price, of course. They snapped my hand off, but to our amazement, the queue at the boot just got bigger and bigger and, some twenty minutes later, I sold the last of the fish and threw in the cool box as well. Goodbye, Fleetwood.

Staying loyal to Fleetwood.

Staley ready to resist approach

By Mike Young

TORN Fleetwood Town manager Phil Staley was today poised to put loyalty ahead of cash and reject a lucrative job elsewhere.

Gainsborough Trinity have targeted Staley to guide them into the Vauxhall Conference, and last night asked him to switch his bid to cling to premier division survival.

But Staley was meeting Town chairman Stuart Kay today hoping to thrash out a deal that he has at the forefront of the bottom club's bid to cling to premier division survival.

One thing, however, was absolutely certain this morn-

ing — Staley will still be at Highbury come Saturday. For Gainsborough now in town have weakened for a match vital to both clubs.

Taking over Trinity would move Staley considerably closer to his goal of handling a Conference club. When appointed, Staley, one of non-League's most respected figures, didn't disguise the hope that getting Town out of trouble could spark Conference attention.

After Trinity approached Mr Kay late last week, Staley met officials of the seventh-placed Lincolnshire outfit last night.

Staley said he had to be fair to himself and see what

Lincolnshire poachers try to sell Conference lure

they had to say. Two factors influenced him — they are, behind Boston United, potentially the second biggest club in the NPL, and are geared for the Conference.

Welsh international Leighton James left Trinity for Morecambe recently after three months in the managerial chair.

"They made me a very attractive offer, but there were one or two points I got a little tight about. And there are other things to be considered", said Staley, who admitted his mind wasn't properly concentrated on the Town team during Saturday's 1-0 win home over Bridlington.

"I have thought a lot about

the situation since the offer was made, and haven't slept very much.

"But Staley doesn't want to walk away from the task of helping lift Town to safety after the deep depression over Highbury before a new regime took over the club in November. He isn't on contract. He was appointed in mid-December until May.

"Trinity's terms were very attractive, but there are times when loyalty must come before finance.

"Staley said he has been overwhelmed by Mr Kay's dedication to the club and determination to keep him.

"Before meeting the chairman today, Staley said "it still looks very much as

though I will stay. Because of my loyalty and a commitment I gave to the fans and club, it would not be nice of me to leave. My word and my bond make we want to carry on."

"He applauded local people for rallying behind Town's rescue act.

"They have been coming out of the doors with the results we've had in my three games."

"Staley said there was no guarantee he and his assistant Harry Dunn could keep the club in the premier division.

"But if we give it our best, at least we know we will have honoured our commitment to the club."

PHIL STALEY ... 'very attractive offer — but there are times when loyalty must come before finance'

Fleetwood
Town with
Harry Dunn
(far right)

Action from Highbury - not Arsenal but Fleetwood!

8

The shortest job in football

It was the quietest pre-season I had ever known. A holiday in the Caribbean followed by weeks enjoying the garden and spending time with the family. For once, I didn't have to worry about shrinking wage bills or scouring the region for up and coming talent. In the midst of this lull in my life, Andrea and I were invited to a party hosted by a good friend of the family. It was a fortieth birthday bash and I knew that there would be a lot of footballers and ex-players there.

However, I did not realise that one of the guests would be the Crewe Alexandra boss Dario Gradi. I had known Dario for several years, and we got talking at the party and I explained that I was due to start the season without a club. Dario suggested I might like to do a bit of scouting for him, and I felt it would be an ideal way of keeping my eye on what was happening in the non-league game.

I had done business with Dario before, having sold

him Tony Naylor from Droylsden and then Martin Clark from Accrington Stanley, so Dario knew I had an eye for good up and coming players. Dario told me his assistant manager Brian Eastpick would ring me the following week to tell me which game he wanted me to cover for the following Saturday, the start of the new season. I was quite thrilled at the prospect of scouting for Crewe; no pressure to get a result, no worries about whether or not your players would turn up and not having to spend all week on the phone as all non-league bosses have to do. I was really looking forward to this new challenge.

The following Tuesday, Brian rang and asked if I would go to watch a young left-sided midfield player at Bamber Bridge called Tom McKenna. Brian had heard from another scout that this young lad was putting in some impressive performances and he wanted a second opinion. My scouting pass was in the post and Brian told me to collect my matchday ticket at the ground when I arrived. Bamber Bridge were playing at home to Workington Town that weekend and I felt it would be a good match, as well.

Bamber Bridge was a two-hour car journey from Cheshire so I gave myself plenty of time and set off. On the way, I called at Charnock Richard Services for a pie and a cup of coffee. On my way back to the car, I heard a gruff voice behind me. A shady looking character was standing in the car park next to a white

Transit van and he asked me if I could spare a minute to look at something that might be of interest to me.

I wandered over and he threw open the side of the van and asked if I was interested in gold ladies and gents watches. I said no, but the guy was very insistent. He said: "What about trying this then?" He opened the back door of the van very slightly and as I peered in I could see a young girl, half-naked, lying on a mattress. I was gobsmacked, as the "pimp" asked if I wanted to have sex with her, for a fee, of course. Sadly, Charnock Richard Services has never seemed to me to be the most erotic venue in the world, so I mumbled something about being short of time and scuttled away to my car.

It was the strangest experience and I considered calling the police, but didn't want to be late for the game at Bamber Bridge so I carried on with my journey. Had I got into the van, would I ever have been seen again? Brian had asked me to put my report into the club on Monday but I decided to omit the Charnock Richard episode and concentrate on the performance of young Tom McKenna.

Over the next few months, I must have visited two dozen grounds, reporting on different players. But if you have ever been involved in scouting for a league club, you will know that it often feels like a lost cause as very few of your targets ever actually end up joining your club. Out of all the players I watched for Crewe, not one of them actually put pen to paper at Gresty Road and, to cap it all, the one player I really rated was allowed to slip through their fingers.

I visited Nuneaton Borough to watch Malcolm Christie and gave this player a glowing report, believing him to be definitely one for the future. Crewe could have signed this lad for just £35,000 but they deliberated for too long and, some six months later in 1998, Derby County steamed in and snapped him up for a bargain £50,000.

The boy has since gone on to play in the Premiership and has represented his country at under-21 level, scoring his first international goal against Greece in May 2001. Christie burst onto the Premiership scene with two goals on his debut in January 2000 and was named Derby's Young Player of the Year that season. Mally went on to score a wonderful individual goal at Old Trafford to secure Premiership status for Jim Smith's side the following year.

But for every one that slips through Dario's net, there are always another two that he brings through his Schoolboy Academy. The man is a genius who has forgotten more about football than the rest of us will ever know.

Then came a bolt out of the blue which would lead to my shortest ever appointment in non-league management. I was contacted by David Pace, the highly eccentric chairman of my former club

Droylsden FC. He asked if he could pop round to discuss the possibility of me returning to the Butcher's Arms. Droylsden were on a very poor run at the time, ten games without a win.

At the time, Dave was new to non-league football and he had installed the late Peter O'Brien as manager at the start of the season. I had known Peter for a good while, both on and off the pitch, and we had had our differences over the years but remained on speaking terms.

My first thought was that Peter, or OB as he was known, must be on a contract, but Dave Pace denied this when he came to see me. He then went on to tell me that he had spoken to OB and told him that he was going to be replaced for Saturday's away trip to Horwich RMI. He went on to tell me his plans for Droylsden and, eventually, I agreed to sign a contract until the end of the season. The signing of the contract was witnessed by the only other person at my house that night - the mother-in-law.

I never had the chance to meet the players before the game, we were simply told what time to meet up at Horwich on Saturday. I rang Tony Keyes, who had played Debbie McGee to my Paul Daniels before! He had previously announced his decision to retire from football, but he agreed to join me once again as my assistant. I met Tony at 1.30pm that Saturday afternoon to head north to Horwich. We chatted in the car, not knowing whether all the lads would turn up, but I knew that if the players were owed wages, then they would definitely be there. Fortunately I knew at least eight of them, anyway, and I knew which of the playing staff had been signed up by Droylsden so I already had a rough idea of the side I wanted to put out at Horwich - if they all turned up.

Tony and I arrived early, as always, and the players started to arrive in dribs and drabs. There was a coach due to arrive from Droylsden, but I had been informed that only a couple of the players would be using it. By two o'clock the squad had assembled and I spoke to them all, keeping it brief, but asked them to do their best and we would sort out any problems at training the following Tuesday. The team was named and I explained the formation I felt would be best with the players I had available.

Then I received the most disturbing news - the former management team was in the crowd and I was warned to expect some abuse. Normally this would be water off a duck's back, but I was still grateful for the warning. The lads battled hard that day and gained a well-earned draw at Horwich, Droylsden's first point for almost a month. Amidst a fair amount of abuse from OB and his cronies, we retired to the dressing room and reminded the lads to report for training on Tuesday.

Having gone through the day without speaking to

the chairman, I was expecting a phone call from Mr Pace on the Sunday, but no call came. On Monday morning I took a couple of calls from two of the players asking what was going on, as they had heard through the grapevine that Peter O'Brien had been reinstated, which left me totally flabbergasted.

Throughout the day I tried repeatedly to contact Dave Pace, but he was doing a very good impression of the Scarlet Pimpernel. Finally, at six o'clock that evening, he rang me to explain that he had dropped a huge clanger. He explained that OB did have a contract, after all. Dave told me that, because of pressure from other anonymous sources, he had decided to reappoint his ex-manager. I later found out that this had all been decided in the pub on Saturday night after the game, but the chairman could not bring himself to sack me until the Monday night. My second spell at Droylsden FC had lasted for 48 hours - and I hadn't even been inside the ground. Mind you, I left them a point better off than when I started.

OB and I remained good friends despite this ridiculous sequence of events and it came as a big shock when I heard he had died. Peter was a tremendous non-league player and gave his all when managing Hyde United, Witton Albion and Droylsden. He has been badly missed in Tameside. Another major disappointment was to lose the services of my great friend Tony Keyes once again, who decided to quit for good after this crazy affair.

After the Christmas holidays, I got a surprise phone call from the Chairman of Congleton Town asking if I would be willing to meet with him and his committee on Tuesday night at Booth Street, Congleton's home ground. I was aware that the manager's job at Congleton had become vacant just a week before this call. As usual, these calls never come when a side is doing well; Congleton Town were bottom of the league. But unlike the situation at Fleetwood, Congleton were not quite so far adrift, as they were only two points behind the team immediately above them in the table. There were twelve games left, eight of them at home, and I felt I could keep them up and prevent them dropping into the North West Counties League, so I accepted their offer to become manager.

Tony Keyes had made it clear he was out of the game for good, so I embarked on a new partnership. Benny Phillips was managing my old side Grove United in the Mid-Cheshire League and I had heard they were doing well, so I felt this might be an opportunity for him to step up and progress his own career in non-league football. Benny accepted my offer and we set about the task of keeping Congleton Town in the HFS Loans League.

The first three of our fixtures were all at home. We held our inaugural training session and decided to play a practice match between the existing players, plus nine new players that Benny and I had managed to round up. It turned out to be a smart move as it gave us the chance to form immediate opinions about the players who could do a job for us.

Taking over at a new club is never easy, because there are players you like and there are others who like themselves and believe they are better than they actually are. Sometimes you'll find certain lads who loved the previous manager and don't want to play for anyone else. Congleton Town was no different. Four of the existing squad threw the towel in straight away, leaving us 18 to choose from.

After taking stock of what was available, Benny told all the players to report to the ground at 2pm the following Saturday for our first game at home to Gretna, the town famous for secret weddings and couples who elope in the night. But Gretna were starting to make a name for themselves on the football field and were riding high in the league.

Benny and I sat in our private changing room, which was ten yards from the main dressing room, and selected the team. The problem of having a separate dressing room is that you have no idea what the lads are saying or thinking, so we needed a spy. Benny had a good pal called Syd Thompson, a local businessman from Wilmslow, who went everywhere with Benny. Syd wanted to be involved on the coaching side so we told him to go and get changed with the players. His job was to keep his eyes and ears open so he could report back to us at the end of the game.

Congleton was a well-staffed club and had its own physio who we also met on our first day in charge. The Secretary told us that the physio would also act as sponge man on match days. But when the physio came in to our changing room, it was no man. Benny had to whip his shorts up rapidly as we met Lena the physio. We invited Lena to use our private changing room to get ready for the match, but she refused and said she would prefer to get changed with the lads. With that, she headed off to the main dressing room, leaving us to get on with the job in hand.

We went over to give our team talk to the players - and Lena - before heading off to take up our seats in the dugout. We got a warm reception from the supporters, all 96 of them, plus the extra six who had travelled down from Gretna.

But the game was electric and an absolute treat for the 102 spectators who had turned out that day. We took a shock lead in the opening quarter of an hour with a great left-footed shot from a young lad I had taken on loan from Crewe Alexandra - Mark Rivers. Mark, of course, went on to have a very successful time with Crewe before a £600,000 move to Norwich City. Gretna's star players were the Armstrong brothers and it was no surprise when Les Armstrong popped up just before the break to level the scoreline.

In the second half, I knew we would have the wind and the slope of the pitch in our favour and I felt we might just nick the points this afternoon. Sure enough, with ten minutes left on the clock, Andy Atkinson, on loan from Macclesfield Town, fired a tremendous shot into the top corner and we held on for a terrific 2-1 victory.

After the match, the atmosphere was amazing and even Gretna's Chairman Jocky Dalglish came up to congratulate us on our victory. But there was another bonus still to come. Benny, me and the Chairman were chatting in our executive Portakabin when Syd Thompson came charging in. He yelled: "Come quickly, you have got to see this!"

We followed him up to the main dressing room and ducked inside one of the cubicles where we perched on top of the toilet seat. Syd was craning his neck to look over the top into the showers next door. Down below was our physio Lena, totally naked, having a shower with all of the players. Syd was actually horrified and refused to go into the showers undressed, so he was finally persuaded to go in with his shorts on. But no sooner had he set foot on the tiled floor than Lena instructed him to take them off. Syd sheepishly did as he was told, to a loud cheer from the rest of the lads.

Lena later told us: "I always shower with the players. If I am going to work with you then I will do the same as everyone else. There's no room for being shy about these things." From that day on, Syd always got changed with me and Benny next door.

It had been a superb day and just the start we would have wished for. Everyone at the club was very friendly, especially the tea ladies who made the most fantastic fresh sandwiches. Over the next few weeks we went from strength to strength picking up twelve points out of a possible 21 and moving Congleton Town out of the drop zone for the first time that season. I had some very useful players pass through our ranks, as well. Mark Rivers, of course, but also Wes Simpson and Mark Ceralo who went on to play at a decent level.

With just two weeks of the season remaining, Benny and I were approached by one of my former chairmen Terry Styring, who had become a good friend during my time at Accrington Stanley. Terry had just taken up the reins at another of my previous clubs, Ashton United, and made me a very attractive offer. There was good money on the table and he was willing to offer me a two-year contract at Ashton in time for the coming season.

Benny and I thought long and hard about the offer and we both agreed that it would be a massive challenge. The money was good, but the people at Congleton had been unbelievable, so friendly all the time. Even after a defeat, the committee were positive and my heart was telling me to stay, even though my wallet was telling me to leave. In the end, I made the wrong decision and opted to return to Ashton United. It was one of the biggest mistakes of my career to leave this amazing little club.

I left behind people who had taken all the stress out of Saturday afternoons but I had allowed the lure of the money to tempt me away. One thing I know now is that big money means people expect big results. The result is the only thing that counts.

When Benny and I took over at Hurst Cross, the home of Ashton United, it didn't take us long to find out what kind of pressure we were going to be under. There had been some big-name non-league managers in the chair before me, who had all finished in the top six, just missing out on promotion each time. People such as Kevin Keelan, Trevor Ross, David Denby and, the biggest of them all, Sammy McIlroy, who went on to work miracles at Macclesfield before taking over as manager of Northern Ireland. All of these guys had been hired and fired by what I called "the drinking club". This was a section of the board of directors who started drinking at twelve noon and usually finished at midnight on match days, talking total crap after the game they had witnessed, and making decisions fuelled by booze. In many ways, I felt they were to blame for the club's lack of progress through the leagues.

Finishing sixth in our first season in charge was

not the outcome that the directors had envisaged for Ashton United. It was a mediocre season by anyone's standards. The only highlight was the way our physio dealt with a particularly nasty broken leg when we played at Lincoln United. For the second time in a row, we found ourselves blessed with a very attractive female physio - sadly Julie Carter wouldn't get in the shower with the lads, but she was one of the best physios I have ever met in my career. On this particular day, our midfield player Ian Boyle went into a tackle and came out with a shocking injury. Julie was magnificent and kept her head when everyone else was losing theirs.

After several disagreements with the board, and far too many defeats for their liking the following season, I became the fifth manager in as many years to suffer the chop. But I can say in all honesty that it turned out to be the best decision the "drinking club" ever made. It was as if they had lifted a 56lb bag of potatoes off my back.

My thoughts at the time were: if they can sack Sammy McIlroy, then it was certainly no disgrace when I was asked to leave the football club. The only difference: Sammy went on to manage Northern Ireland while I ended up at Caernarvon Town in the Welsh League.

Sacked by Ashton United - just like Sammy McIlroy!

Talent spotting for Dario!

Benny Phillips my number two at Ashton United and Congleton Town.

Boardroom and Manager's Office at Congleton.

The new stand at Congleton.

9

Hungary for success

Being out of work again at Christmas meant I could relax more than ususal, have a few drinks whenever I wanted and not have to worry about picking up players. But, when it's in your blood you are always hoping that the phone might ring with a decent offer. Sure enough, I didn't have to wait very long, but this time it was a different kind of offer.

I had always been the number one at my previous clubs, barring a short spell as assistant manager at Chorley, but this time an old pal of mine Steve Joel rang to say he had taken the manager's job at Caernarvon Town in the new Football League of Wales. He asked if I would be willing to go and help him, and I felt it would be a great opportunity to get involved in football once again.

Steve suggested that we should meet at a sauna, of all places, in the Kensington area - that's Liverpool, not London! Kensington is a real rough end of town twinned with Kandahar, I believe. I met Steve outside this dodgy-looking venue covered in graffiti and with windows barred. Inside it was even worse. It was like entering the Dark Ages, and I hardly dared hang my clothes up in case the hook fell out of the wall.

Inside the sauna were another twenty blokes squeezed into a tiny space, but we squashed in and started to sweat. After quarter of an hour we decided to move on to the jacuzzi which was already occupied by five Scousers. They were each clutching a water bottle, like all good athletes. But we later discovered each bottle contained eight-year-old Bell's Whiskey. And the more drunk they got, the noisier they became, and it prevented us from starting our discussions about the task at Caernarvon.

It was no surprise when the manager of the sauna eventually came over and asked three of the lads to hand over their bottles. But he certainly wasn't expecting one of their pals to grab hold of him and yank him into the jacuzzi with them, fully dressed with suit and tie for good measure. The guy began to panic at this point because he had visions of drowning as he went under for the fifth time. It seemed like a good time to disappear to the rest room. The remainder of the staff looked to be on the verge of calling the police.

The rest of the whiskey drinkers headed for the sauna eventually - we knew they had gone in because we saw everyone else coming out en masse. But the situation was about to turn nasty, as one of the lunatics decided to pour some of his whiskey over the top of the hot coals, which immediately caught fire and it wasn't too long before flames were licking their way around the wooden structure.

Steve and I rushed to get changed and headed for the exit doors, but we were held up by the police and fire brigade who had arrived on the scene. After asking us a few questions, we were allowed to leave and decided to hold our meeting elsewhere. Steve's Player/Coach Alan McDonald lived nearby so we decided to discuss the future there.

Alan had played for a variety of clubs during his career, so I was well aware of his pre-match ritual, which normally consisted of a few puffs on the wacky-baccy and a pint of lager. But, I have to say, he was a great lad, and the three of us sat down, had a good chat and I decided to give it a go at Caernarvon.

Our aim was to get the club into the top three, which would result in a place in the Intertoto Cup, a competition much-maligned by the Premiership sides in England, but a tournament which represented a vital lifeline for the League of Wales. It offers a unique opportunity to draw a major European club side and bring in much-needed revenue and attract a good deal of media attention.

Steve knew the existing staff at Caernarvon but asked if I could come up with three decent players to add to the squad. Our first fixture would be away at Carmarthen Town, and I was finding it difficult to persuade players to travel from my neck of the woods to play a game of football. But eventually I acquired three lads who I knew pretty well and asked them to join me on this journey into the unknown.

Greg Hepolite was a striker from the Moss Side district of Manchester, midfielder Warren Thompson was the son of Syd Thompson who worked with me at Congleton and the trio was completed by wide man Neil Ogden from Wigan. Steve Joel rang me on Thursday night two days before the game to give me the news that we would be meeting at the unearthly time of 7am on Saturday morning at the Chester Post House Hotel. Now I realised what I was letting myself in for.

After a journey of five-and-a-half hours, we were still ten miles away from our final destination, eating beans on toast in a Little Chef. The reality was starting to hit home as I managed to find a map of Wales and started to recall the vastness of this country and the lack of any decent roads.

However, we made a good start: we won the game 3-1 with a magnificent hattrick from Greg Hepolite and Steve was absolutely delighted with my new signing. The talk on the bus during the long trip back to Chester was all about how well the team had knitted together, considering this was the first time most of these lads had met each other. Some of them were already dreaming of European competition.

The Camarthen manager that afternoon was a friend of mine from my days at Bangor City, John Mahoney, the former Welsh international midfielder. He spent most of the day drooling over young Hepolite's hattrick and I am sure if the lad would have been willing to travel that far south every week, then John would have been offering good money for him.

The next few weeks saw Caernarvon rise from tenth in the league to the top four and everyone at the club started to get excited about the prospect of finishing in the top three and qualifying for a dream ticket to Europe. But every week the away trips seemed to get longer, leaving early in the morning and hoping desperately that the players would make it to the allotted pick-up point.

On one particular occasion, we were playing away at Barry Town which is down near Cardiff and we arrived at the Lord Daresbury Hotel to meet three players from Liverpool who were travelling with us to Chester for an 8am rendezvous with the team coach. It was a wet and windy morning as this blue Escort pulled into the car park with just two people inside. A lad called Mike Quigley was missing and it transpired he had become involved in a bit of a skirmish the night before. As a result, he had been offered a night's free accommodation at the local police station, which meant we would be travelling to South Wales a man down.

This was the big problem with non-league players; if they didn't show up you couldn't fine them because they would just stop playing altogether. The simplest way out was normally to make sure one of your backroom staff was also registered as a player just in case of emergencies, but we didn't have that luxury. Our trip to Barry was embarrassing as we were well and truly turned over losing 4-0, and it felt like an extremely long journey home.

Although we were short on players, we were never short on characters at the football club and our groundsman Bob was one of the best. I knew he was a keen fisherman and, after my experiences at Fleetwood, I got onto the subject quite easily. Bob told me that the River Ogwen, which runs through the mountains above the ground, was packed with salmon and Bob said he would fetch some for me.

True to his word, the following week Bob produced a big black bin liner containing a beautiful two-foot long red salmon - it cost me just two pints of lager. Cutting this fish into steaks became a weekly ritual and soon my freezer at home was so full it couldn't hold any more. To be honest, meal times became a bit repetitive.

Despite our setback at Barry, the team kept on picking up points and I kept on picking up fish. We maintained our place in the league table but crashed out of the Welsh Cup away to Ebbw Vale. They also became only the second side to beat us in the league, which allowed them to leapfrog above us in the table.

With three games remaining, we knew we had to win all three to finish in the top three and qualify for Europe. Ebbw Vale set themselves exactly the same task as it came down to a two-horse race for the final European spot. They had the better goal difference, so we needed them to slip up. We won our next two games against Conwy and Caerws (I still can't pronounce that name). Ebbw Vale also won their next two fixtures and the scene was set for a grandstand finish.

Ebbw Vale played their final game the night before us, and the news came through that they had lost - our fate was in our own hands at last. We were up against Connahs Quay in our last game, knowing that a draw would now be enough to earn a place in the Intertoto Cup the following July. To pile even more pressure on, the draw for the qualifying round was actually made on the morning of our game - our opposition would be a crack side from Budapest in Hungary. The tension was too much.

Connahs Quay wasn't too far to travel, for once, but anyone who knows the ground will tell you it has a huge slope from one end to the other. In fact, they would be better to cover it in snow and use it for downhill skiing events. Most of our lads had never set foot outside of the UK so the thought of a trip to Hungary was weighing heavily on their minds but it was also a terrific incentive. The pre-match team talk would take care of itself.

We met at 5.30pm that Wednesday evening, with only Warren Thompson to collect on the way, because all the other players were making their own way to the ground. It's difficult to explain the thoughts that were going through my head that day as we headed over to Connahs Quay, which seemed a long way from Hungary, a country that I had never expected to be visiting in my lifetime. I felt even more nervous than when I had ever been as a player.

With a fully fit squad to select from, Steve decided to stick with the lads who had served the team so well for most of the time we had been in charge, rather than making changes for the sake of it. At five to seven, the lads took to the field and there was nothing else we could do.

We lost the toss, which was always a blow at Connahs Quay, because it meant the home side could play up the slope in the first half, but play downhill in the second. I felt we would have to go in at the break with at least a two-goal lead, because this slope really does play a big part at Connahs Quay. But, after just nine minutes, we conceded a corner and the home side went in front with a thunderous header, giving our keeper no chance whatsoever. To this day, I am convinced my heart stopped ticking for a second or two.

Our opponents were up for this game, chasing, harrassing and giving 100% all over the park. But remembering we only needed a point, the lads didn't panic and kept their shape in the hope we could at least nick a goal from somewhere. But half time came and we were still one-nil down and, as I walked off the pitch, I could see Ebbw Vale's manager and his assistant in the crowd with big smiles on their faces.

We knew it would be difficult in the second half playing up the slope, but Steve just told the lads to keep their work rate up and hopefully they would get their reward. I went round the changing room speaking to each of the lads, reminding them of the prize up for grabs at the end of ninety minutes. The more I spoke about the prospect of Hungary in June, the more I felt the butterflies in my stomach.

I crossed my fingers, my toes, my legs, everything, as we took to the field for the most important 45 minutes of my career. The crowd was ten times bigger than normal for Connahs Quay, swelled by a tremendous following of 800 fans from Caernarvon.

On 51 minutes we won a free kick on the edge of the opposition penalty area and up stepped our leading goalscorer Eiffion Williams, better known to the lads as Ted. He placed the ball and curled a wonderful right-footed shot into the top corner of the net, but just as he spun away to celebrate, I spotted the linesman had lifted his flag. The referee went over to consult with him for the most incredibly tense few seconds I have ever experienced in football. Then, to our amazement, the ref awarded a free kick to Connahs Quay. I sprinted up the touchline to the linesman to ask him why he had disallowed the goal. He said: "Offside." I said: "Bollocks." The official then waved his flag again to attract the attention of the referee, while I continued to use every word in my 'swear word dictionary' in a volley of abuse at the linesman.

In the midst of my tirade, I seem to remember suggesting that he was biased towards the home side because most of them were local Welsh lads, I certainly used the word "cheat". We had just one Welsh guy in our starting eleven and I suggested that this had influenced his decision. To wind me up even further, the linesman answered back in Welsh. Eventually, I was sent to the stands for the 14th time in my career and I knew we had been cheated out of a perfectly good goal. It seemed so unfair on the lads after the tremendous effort they had put in.

Steve managed to calm me down, pointing out that there was still plenty of time to get the equaliser, so I took my seat in the stands. But after 75 minutes there was still no sign of a breakthrough, as their keeper continued to perform miracles to keep us at bay. Steve decided to give it a last throw of the dice, bringing on another striker and taking off a defender with just ten minutes to go.

Neil Ogden had an instant impact as he raced clear of their defenders and everyone in the ground rose to their feet as we wondered if this would be the moment that would clinch our place in Europe. But Neil decided not to blast the ball, and instead tried to dribble round the keeper. He knocked the ball past the goalie but, as he went past him, the keeper flung himself at Neil and brought him crashing down inside the box - a clear penalty.

But incredibly the referee waved play on. Our entire bench rose to their feet and charged onto the pitch to protest. The ref had to halt the game while he tried to restore order. After five minutes of argy-bargy the officials still couldn't calm Caernarvon down and, eventually, the police became involved and managed to persuade our subs and coaching staff to go back to the dug out. The game restarted, but it was too late for us, as Connahs Quay held on and ran out 1-0 winners, shattering our dreams of playing in Europe.

But the story doesn't end there because the officials continued to be harrassed and abused as they left the pitch and somehow one supporter managed to get into the referee's changing room and dumped his clothes into the toilet before flushing the chain. Despite one or two fingers pointing in my direction,

I can categorically state that the offender certainly wasn't me. I would have flushed the ref down the loo, not just his clothes.

Our dressing room was shrouded in a deathly hush after the final whistle, the players with their heads in their hands and there were a few tears, as well. As Warren and I headed out to the car park for the journey home, we had more salt rubbed in our wounds when we saw the managers of Ebbw Vale and Connahs Quay outside the main entrance shaking hands with one another. It left us feeling sick, but instead of heading for Budapest in Hungary, we were hungry and headed for the nearest KFC.

The disappointment was immense, but this great game of football has a habit of lifting you from the depths of despair and you have to dust yourself down and start again. In the immediate aftermath of this game it was difficult to see any light at the end of the tunnel, but within a few days all the talk was about next season and another crack at Europe.

Steve decided we needed to stengthen our squad for the coming season so we set about talking to a couple of new prospects in the hope that we would be able to persuade them to travel some 200 miles every Saturday. It was no easy task, but we did attract a couple of new faces and arranged four pre-season fixtures nearer to home so we could break them in.

But our preparations suffered a blow when we played

my local side Poynton FC in a friendly on a wet and windy Tuesday night. I took my seat next to Steve in the dugout to keep out of the rain, but fifteen minutes into the game, leading 2-0, I let my enthusiasm get the better of me once again. A decision went against us and I launched my fist into the air, forgetting about the low, wooden roof immediately above us. My fist smashed into the roof and I dislocated my index and middle fingers so badly that I had to go to hospital - after the match, of course.

Sadly, I was joined in the casualty department by one of our lads, Mick Brown, who had unfortunately suffered a hairline fracture of his right leg. I still remember this night well, because we forced poor Mick to play on for eight minutes before we realised how serious his injury was. But at least we were able to hold each other's hands while waiting some two hours for treatment. Obviously I had to use the hand that wasn't broken.

We played a further three friendlies before making arrangements for the first game of the new season away to Aberystwyth Town. We decided to use cars for this trip rather than a coach to make it easier to get straight home after the match. Steve decided to pick up in Liverpool and I thought the Lord Daresbury Hotel would be best for the Manchester-based players, just off the M56. But, as usual, you are always on pins until every player arrives. Sure enough, one of our new additions, Richard Batho, failed to show. After numerous telephone calls, we decided to travel without him. Thankfully, we had managed to register one of our back room staff as a player to plug any gaps.

Richard, who lived in Staffordshire, had been registered as a Caernarvon player on the previous Thursday so I was shocked after losing 3-0 to hear that Richard Batho had decided to spend the afternoon playing for Kidsgrove Athletic at Burscough FC, instead. He scored a hat trick in a three-all draw. It was a decision that would later cost Kidsgrove heavily because Richard was already registered with another club when he turned out for the Staffordshire outfit.

During the following week I received a telephone call from Steve Joel explaining that his wife was about to go into hospital for a serious operation, so he had decided to resign as manager of Caernarvon. My chin hit the floor, because we had begun to forge a good relationship and I felt we were on course to achieve the goals we had set out to achieve at the start of the season. Later that evening I received another phone call from Club Secretary John Watkins who asked me to attend a board meeting at Caernarvon the following day.

By the end of that meeting, I had been offered only the role of Caretaker Manager, which I have to say came as a big disappointment given my track record. But I accepted it, anyway, although it turned out to be a poisoned chalice. After six league games, we had managed two wins and two draws, but we had also reached the second round of the Welsh Cup with a 6-0 win over Chirk. I felt this was a good time to demand a contract until the end of the season in order to build on a reasonably solid base. But my request was rejected.

It was time to walk away, although it gave me no pleasure to see Caernarvon relegated to the Gwynedd League in the following season. They did bounce back into the League of Wales recently, and I was delighted for the supporters because it is without doubt one of the friendliest clubs in the principality.

I had worked in North Wales on three separate occasions and built up strong relationships with a lot of people there during my career. The travelling was a total pain in the arse, often quite literally in the days before the Chirk bypass, when bumpy, pot-holed minor roads were the only option available. But I will always remember the good times in North Wales with people who just loved football. My management career started in Wales and it finished there, too. And I'll never forget eating that freshwater salmon.

Groundsman Bob brought me fish from here - the River Ogwen.

Caernarvon Town.

Storm clouds gather over Caernarvon.

Get Those Sheep Off The Pitch! - Phil Staley

10

Taking the Mic

After 26 years of involvement in non-league football I finally decided to call it a day, but soon discovered there is nothing worse then sitting at home on a Saturday afternoon. I wondered just how long it might be before something took my fancy. I was discussing this one day with my son Steven and he explained that my local radio station in Stockport, Signal FM, were looking for someone to provide the analysis on all of Stockport County's fixtures, home and away, alongside their sports editor Jon Keighren.

Steven spoke to Jon and fixed up a meeting at the station and I went down to discuss the vacant position. I did have some radio experience - well, I switched one on in Curry's once!

I remember vividly driving down to Signal to meet Jon because, on the way, this battered old van turned into Heaton Lane where the station was based. Suddenly it lost its near side passenger door - it just fell off completely and smashed to the floor, scattering pedestrians in its midst and leaving the driver with a look of sheer panic on his face. It was the funniest thing I had seen for a while and I walked into the building with tears rolling down my cheeks.

I met Steve in the reception area and he took me through to meet Jon for the very first time. I remember I had built up a picture of Jon in my mind after hearing him so many times on the radio, but I can tell you the real thing was a million miles away from my mental image. This compact figure with his head completely shaved rose from his leather-clad executive chair to greet me and straight away I had visions of a young Jim Smith - the Bald Eagle!

Jon shook my hand and welcomed me to Signal FM and proceeded to introduce me to Station Manager Denise Mickle who was working to attract a sponsor for the show. Little did I know that Denise and her partner Ed James, then presenter of the Breakfast Show, were to become very good friends over the next few years. Jon also introduced me to the Programme Controller Mark Chivers, a lovely guy who was very keen for the sports show to work.

Jon and I agreed to give it a couple of games to see how it went and we arranged to meet on Saturday next for the season opener away to Bradford City at Valley Parade. When we pulled up outside the ground, Jon handed me a polo shirt with the Signal FM logo emblazoned across the front. It was the most hideous item of clothing imaginable, but to loud cheers from the passing supporters I got changed in the street. Well, it was August and it was a pretty warm day, after all. With my 56-year-old frame, there wasn't much danger of women swooning.

The next 90 minutes were to become the start of a long working relationship between Jon and myself and we became the best of friends as a result. It was also the start of witnessing many exciting games, as well as a string of hilarious incidents over the next couple of years. Our programme, Signal SuperSport, was an instant hit with the fans. It ran from two till six every Saturday, and seven till ten for midweek games.

The away trips were particularly eventful and tremendous fun, as we often stayed over with the County players and officials on longer trips. County's Marketing Manager Steve Bellis was always excellent company on the long journeys and kept us entertained - and he always had a good supply of Midget Gems to keep us going.

The County players came to trust us and we often gave them a laugh on the longer trips. I remember one game down at Norwich City when full back Sean Connelly had fallen out with manager Gary Megson. Megson, a strong manager and a tough character, decided to drop Connelly to the bench. It was a bold decision by the gaffer as Connelly had been virtually a permanent fixture in the side.

But Sean Connelly thought the whole thing was laughable and couldn't resist waving up at us in the Main Stand at Carrow Road as he warmed up along the touchline during the game. He then proceeded to turn around so we could see the number twelve on his back and pointed at it. Megson would have gone ballistic if he had spotted this exchange.

From an entertainment point of view, the commentaries were getting better each week, so much so that the station manager asked us to introduce a post-match phone-in after every game. I took charge of this section of the show and thoroughly enjoyed it, as each week I invited a different player to join me on-air for that final hour, while Jon went off to get his post-match interviews.

The beauty of a radio phone-in is that you never quite know what's coming next. On one occasion, we had a call from a guy called Ted Lettuce, who made some very random points. Ted became something of a regular and had a very unique character and a very distinctive voice. The fans used to love hearing Ted's views, which sometimes strayed into surreal territory. One week he suggested that Edgeley Park should be turned into a real park, with some swings and a slide for the children. It was several weeks later when we found out that Ted Lettuce was in fact a pseudonym and the calls were being orchestrated by a chap called

Martin Bellis, Steve's brother, who now dresses up every week as County's mascot Vernon Bear.

But I just love talking about football, at any level, and our first season went very well. During the summer, we were both re-employed for the following year and the fans and the players themselves had really taken the show to their hearts.

As the new season got under way, one of our first away trips was the long journey down to Portsmouth, so Jon decided it would be best for us to stay over with the first team at their south coast hotel, the Meon Valley. But he wasn't daft - Jon had already worked out that we would be able to play nine holes on the hotel golf course in the morning before the game.

We had a great morning in the sun and the fresh air before heading off to Fratton Park for the game - but it turned out to be a bad day for County who lost 2-0. However, for me and Jon, the day was about to improve a hundred percent. With the sun still beating down strongly, we began to drive away from Fratton Park in a slow-moving line of traffic. Suddenly, coming towards us on the other side of the road, I spotted a vision. It was the most attractive young lady riding a bike. She was wearing a pair of shorts and the most amazing loose-fitting vest top that left absolutely nothing to the imagination.

I quickly wound down my window as she rode closer and she gave me the biggest grin I have ever seen. I didn't know what to say, so I just yelled out: "That is magnificent!" Jon was in stitches, because I had failed to spot her young daughter in the baby seat - and her huge husband on the bike behind.

The stopovers were always the most eventful occasions with Jon. One time we stayed with the team at a hotel just outside Bristol before County played Bristol City. We always enjoyed a laugh with County's coach driver who was a font of useless information and whose sense of direction was hopeless. Jon and I met him in the hotel lobby on the morning of the game and Jon asked him for directions to the ground as we were going to drive in ourselves. The coach driver said: "Oh, it's really easy - just follow signs for the City Centre, keep the river on your right and keep your eye out for the big red roof." We ended up in the car park of the local B&Q.

It is easy to forget that away trips can be quite boring and repetitive for the first team players who find themselves with a lot of spare time and very little to do. One of our favourites was big Brett Angell who was a legend among County supporters during his two spells with the club scoring 70 goals in 180 games. But in between he did have a rather bad time of it at Premiership Everton where he struggled to make an impact. I used to spend a lot of time telling Everton jokes to keep a smile on Brett's face.

I told him about the Everton souvenir shop that sells

Everton tablecloths: they're quite expensive and they tend to slip down the table after a while. And for the ladies, the Everton bra: comes in the team colours but has little support and is no good in the cups. And, of course, the world famous Everton mints, to help take away the bitter taste of another defeat.

Many of our friendships with these players have lasted over the years. County legend Jim Gannon is still a good friend - Jon and I compered at his testimonial dinner and Jim even joined us on Jon's stag weekend in Jim's home city of Dublin. Former Stockport County keeper Carlo Nash was another big favourite. Carlo, now with Manchester City, has been to Jon's wedding and to my son's wedding, as well - he must love sponge cake!

As well as football, I am a big fan of cricket and never miss the Stockport County charity match organised by the Fingerpost Travel Club every summer. The event sees a current County eleven take on a team made up of ex-players and I have been fortunate enough to turn out for the ex-players on several occasions. (I did make one appearance for County reserves, you know!)

One year, a young striker called Michael Hennessey agreed to play. Michael was a useful footballer and had a terrific sense of humour - but coming from Ireland meant he didn't have a clue about cricket, but he was prepared to give it a bash.

I started to worry when I saw Michael in the pavilion, getting his pads on ready to bat. He couldn't work out how to put the pads on and kept trying to fasten the straps at the front. Every time he stood up, they fell off and poor Michael just couldn't work it out. He looked like a confused contestant during the mental agility round on the Krypton Factor. Not surprisingly, he didn't last long at the crease.

Then it was the turn of the ex-players to bat, so Michael went out to field in the covers. In came former County defender Bill Williams to open the batting and I knew that Bill was a useful cricketer. As the first ball came to Bill, I knew straight away where it was headed. Without hesitation Bill drove the ball superbly out into the covers at a real rate of knots. It was skimming along the ground towards poor Michael.

Anyone else would've let it go, or perhaps dived full length to try and catch it. Not Michael. He decided to use his footballing abilities to trap it! This corkie was flying along at 70mph when Michael stuck out his leg to "control" the ball. You could hear the crack off his shin in the middle of Manchester.

Michael didn't dare admit how much it hurt and, with tears welling in his eyes and his teeth firmly gritted together, he returned the ball to the wicketkeeper before hopping out towards the boundary. I have to confess, I was rolling about laughing as this poor little

Irishman hobbled about in the field. He didn't do it again.

But most of the people involved in football at this level are natural sportsmen and can turn their hand to just about anything. Former County boss Andy Kilner himself was a junior international at cricket and could have player professionally. But he chose football and it turned out to be the right decision, I am sure.

During this particular season, one of our longest away trips took us down to Ipswich over the Christmas holidays, so the County management team decided to make the most of the stopover. They managed to organise a football match against a local Sunday League side in the grounds of the beautiful Five Lakes hotel in Suffolk. Jon Keighren was invited to play in a side that contained some wonderful players - Andy Kilner himself, Assistant Manager Dave Moss, Youth Team Coach Nige Deeley, Physio Roger Wylde and Masseur Kev Scarborough - all of whom had played at a high level. And then there was Rick the Chef in goal!

At my age, I decided my best option would be to referee the game. Rick had a quiet afternoon as the County side dominated from start to finish, and it was an easy one to referee - except for one guy who caused me a few problems...Andy Kilner himself!

Andy moaned and complained from first whistle to last and, when he was tripped outside the box, I thought he was going to launch this poor young lad into orbit. It was interesting to see how competitive Andy was that day, even in a friendly, as the County side ran out 4-0 winners. In many ways, it gives you an insight into the nature of someone who is determined to succeed, whatever the circumstances. Andy, of course, worked miracles to keep County in Division One for two seasons before losing the backing of the fans - and losing his job to Carlton Palmer.

On air, our programme was going well and we had built up a big profile and a big audience. But then, as so often happens, there were changes. The station was sold to new owners who had their own ideas about how things should be run. The old management were swept out and a new team put in their place and they announced that they would now be targetting a predominantly female audience, which they claimed meant there was no place in the schedule for football.

The supporters were up in arms when the news came out about the plans to ditch the show and petitions were launched and protest meetings were held. I could not believe the response. An Action Group was formed to fight back against the new owners and eventually the station did a U-turn. Sport was reinstated, but sadly without the duo of Keighren and Staley. They decided to bring in a female commentator instead, and once again I was looking for pastures new.

Jon was promoted within the organisation, but he

later left radio to pursue a career in PR, although he has since returned to commentate once again on Stockport County. I also stayed with the group, moving to Signal Radio in Stoke-on-Trent to cover Port Vale games while Sports Editor Simon Humphreys went into hospital for an operation. In the space of two months I covered four thousand miles for Signal Radio including Bournemouth and Cambridge, reporting on the ups and downs of Brian Horton's barmy army.

I enjoyed my time in the Potteries immensely. A good friend of mine, Johnny Owen, a very experienced presenter, was back in the studio anchoring the whole show. One particular programme sticks in my mind; it was a day when Arsenal were playing Everton and Johnny handed over to the reporter at the match. As the guy gave his report on the game you could hear the Arsenal fans in the background. They were singing loudly to their rivals. To the tune of You Are My Sunshine, it went:

You are a Scouser, an ugly Scouser,

You're only happy on Giro Day,

Your mum's out thieving, your dad's drug dealing,

So please don't take my hubcaps away.

Johnny somehow kept a straight face and moved on. Sadly, all good things come to an end and, as Simon returned to fitness, I found myself back on the subs' bench, covering odd games when other reporters couldn't get there. But suddenly I got a call out of the blue from Meridian TV asking if I would be interested in working on their Saturday afternoon programme on ITV2 called Football First. Simon had given them an excellent reference and I was very grateful to him.

The co-ordinator, a girl called Rachel, offered me a game from Division Two: Bury v Bournemouth at Gigg Lane on the following Saturday. I was delighted to accept and I have to admit to an attack of the butterflies. This was national television.

Rachel explained that all the technical equipment I needed would be sent to me via a courier service and that she would book a press pass for me at Bury Football Club. Then all I had to do was find the TV point inside the ground, plug in and start work. Sounded easy. But I have to admit I was slightly worried about the technical side of the job - in fact, I still can't programme my video so this box of tricks would clearly be beyond me. I contacted my good friend Jon Keighren and he turned up to help me with a dummy run.

On the day of the game, I did a quick sound check and was told that my first report would be at ten past three. It was a proud moment when I heard the studio presenter Johnny Gould in my headphones giving me my cue to go on: "Now, to the second division game between Bury who are lying fifteenth in the league against Bournemouth who are one place above them.

Covering this game for Football First, Phil Staley." It is at that point I discovered the colour of adrenalin - it is brown! I have to admit I have never been so nervous before in my life after so many years involved in this great game. I was on live television and my name was there on the screen for the nation to see.

Thankfully it went like clockwork and it has to be one of the proudest moments of my life. Every time a goal was scored, my instructions were to contact the studio with the details and prepare to go live. But the goals came thick and fast for my TV debut. As I dialled in to inform the studio that Bournemouth had scored, they rattled in a second from the same player, James Hayter. To make matters worse, as I was giving my live report, up popped Hayter again for his hat trick. My first assignment for ITV2, and I had a hat trick live on air.

It was fantastic after this update to hear the producer in my headphones, Mark Schofield, congratulating me on a job well done. It was a cracking game with three more goals still to come; two more for Bournemouth and one for poor old Bury. I was well pleased with my TV debut and felt more confident as the season went on.

These days, you see so many ex-players reinventing themselves as media pundits or commentators. It means the chances for someone like myself to find work in such a competitive market would always be tough. But, with a bit of help from my close friends, a chunk of good luck and the willingness to accept a new challenge I felt I had achieved something in my life by switching from non-league manager to national TV reporter. As Jon Keighren said to me, full match commentary is easy - you've got all the time in the world to say what you see as it happens. But to squeeze a match report into a concise but detailed thirty seconds takes a lot of skill and normally years of practice.

At the end of my first season I was delighted to hear the news that my services had been retained for the forthcoming campaign. But just a few weeks into the season came a real body blow. ITV Digital had massively overspent on gaining the Nationwide TV rights and were starting to panic. They later admitted they could not afford to meet the terms of their contract, sending dozens of clubs into financial peril while ITV Digital themselves struggled to attract decent viewing figures. For one televised game between Birmingham City and Nottingham Forest there were 17,000 people inside the ground but only 1,000 watching the game on TV.

Consequently, they had to cut costs and a new programme was introduced called The Goal Rush, but ITV had drastically reduced the number of freelance reporters they were using. Producer Mark Schofield told me, along with dozens of others, that regular games were no longer a possibility, as they reverted to using their own staff to cover fewer matches.

Today I am fortunate in that I have built up so many contacts in the game and in the media and I have been able to get some more radio work, which keeps me involved with football on a Saturday afternoon. For someone like me, there is nothing worse than sitting at home whilst games are being played all over the country. I am also doing a lot of after dinner speaking and some compering at various functions and sportsmens' dinners, which I thoroughly enjoy.

I have been involved in the national game for most of my life now, never earning a lot of money from it, but I can honestly say I wouldn't have changed one minute of it. I have lived for football, often at the expense of my family, since the age of six when my father bought me my first ever ball for Christmas. You will understand how long ago it was, because the ball had laces up the side. He also bought me some boots, which were all-leather, including the studs, almost like rugby boots.

I still remember traipsing back from the muddy fields as a kid, leaving the filthy ball outside the back door hoping it would dry out and the mud would flake off. The next day I woke up and rushed outside to find there had been a hard frost overnight and my brand-new ball was now rock hard and shaped like an egg. I was tempted to take up rugby instead, but thankfully my dad replaced the ball a couple of weeks later.

I have decided not to go back into non-league management, for now. Those days are behind me, but it is a career I would recommend to anyone who has the same passion for the game that I have held for 55 years. And who knows, if the right job comes along, maybe I would go back. But the important thing is to always enjoy what you are trying to achieve, because otherwise it is a long time to be unhappy.

The End?

Me and Martin Edwards at Old Trafford. "If you don't shake my hand I'll take my ball home!"

John Keighren might let me get a word in soon!

Keeping goal
for Radio
Manchester at
Old Trafford.

Former County 'keeper Carlo Nash with me and Jon.

With Jon Keighren at Edgeley Park

Above: Eldest son Nicholas, youngest son Steven and daughter Lauren Kate.

Right: My wife Andrea taking another football enquiry!

Got a book in you?

victorpublishing.co.uk

This book is published by Victor Publishing.

Victor Publishing specialises in getting new and independent writers' work published worldwide in both paperback and Kindle format.

If you have a manuscript for a book of any genre (fiction, non-fiction, autobiographical, biographical or even reference or photographic/ illustrative) and would like more information on how you can get your work published and on sale to the general public, please visit us at:

www.victorpublishing.co.uk

Printed in Great Britain
by Amazon

73277671R00142